The
Flying Gourmet

Just Plane Good

The Flying Gourmet

JUST PLANE GOOD

by Marlene B. Morris, CFII

Cover Illustration By Steven Morillo

M & M Publications, New Orleans

Dedication

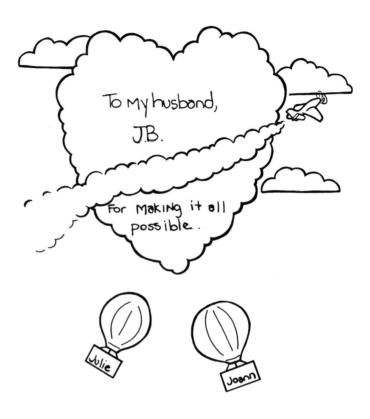

To my husband, J.B.

For making it all possible.

Julie

Joann

Copyright © 1988 By Marlene B. Morris

All rights reserved

'Library of Congress Catalog Number:' 88-90622

International Standard Book Number 0-9620398-0-2

Text Illustration by Ronald L. Smith

Back Cover Photograph by Will Crocker

Printed in the United States of America

Rau's Ex-Cel Printery, Inc.
1716 Franklin Avenue
Gretna, Louisiana 70053

First Printing May 1988

Foreword

Flying is fun and keeps one on the go. Sometimes the food this lifestyle offers is not the nutritious food our Mom and Dad ensured.

I like to think of picnics related to travel. I never get into anything that moves without something to eat, chew or drink. The bottom line – it must be portable, survivable and easy to eat. The recipes in this book accomplish this objective beautifully and still taste 'disgustingly wonderful'. This has been a real challenge and my first beginning.

My experience in cooking is limited to thirty years of taste and error. The recipes were tested and compiled from family favorites of friends and relatives. Recipes are also included from restaurants where pilots frequently dine.

Being somewhat an adventuresome "spirit" I "took" to flying six years ago. While crossing "Ole Smokey" at 10,000 feet, two years ago, munching on Sunshine Chicken and Persimmon Pudding; the idea of **The Flying Gourmet** was born. So being the alert and resourceful pilot which I am, I decided to share my recipes in a cookbook; a book in which my pilot friends can find new ways with food for travel.

As a pilot you will spend about half your life eating away from home. I hope the recipes presented here will help make this experience more convenient, delightful and nutritious for you. Hopefully you will experiment and improve them to your taste and make them your own.

Just Plane Good Wishes,

Since my whirlwind, ten-month, successful campaign for State Treasurer of Louisiana, I have come to more fully appreciate the convenience of air travel and the art of eating on the run. I realize now that there are two essential ingredients to a successful statewide campaign: One is a good pilot and a reliable plane; the other is knowing when and what to eat in between the hundreds of engagements scheduled during a week. A good pilot keeps the candidate on time and sensible eating habits keep the candidate's engine running.

The **Flying Gourmet** offers many delightful recipes that are both delicious as well as nutritious. The following pages are chocked full of recipes that all busy folks can appreciate. I know that you will enjoy soaring to new heights with these unique recipes.

My hat is off to the *Flying Gourmet*!

Mary Landrieu
State Treasurer of Louisiana

ACKNOWLEDGMENTS

vii

Contents

PREFLIGHT APPETIZERS

INFLIGHT HORS d'OEUVRES

LESSON PLAN – MUSHROOM CHANDELLE ROLLS

OBJECTIVE:
To develop the student cook's organization and control of choices while varying ingredients and correction for SCORCH.

ELEMENTS:
Recipe selection, timing, mixture control, roll-out, Scorch control, level off and recovery measures.

SCHEDULE:
Discussion, Demonstration, Practice and Critique.

EQUIPMENT:
Galley, Basic Standard Certified Equipment, Standard Operating Procedure Manual (**The Flying Gourmet,** "Just Plane Good"), Hallon Fire Extinguisher

ACTIONS:
Discuss objective and elements of successfully completing a Mushroom Chandelle.

COMPLETION STANDARDS:
Student cook should demonstrate competency in getting it all together. The entire Mushroom Chandelle should be consistent with the recipe and pass the practical standards BEEFEATER TEST.

Sky Hook Oyster Dip

1 cup shallots, chopped finely
1 large onion, chopped finely
2 garlic cloves, minced
2 tablespoons parsley
1 stick margarine
2 pints raw oysters, well drained
2 sticks butter, unsalted
8 tablespoons flour, all-purpose
2½ cups water
2 tablespoons herb seasoning
½ teaspoon salt
¼ teaspoon black pepper
dash Tabasco
1 box seasoned croutons, crushed

Saute shallots, onions, garlic and parsley with margarine in iron skillet. Add oysters and cook for 3 minutes. Remove from skillet and set aside in large bowl. Melt butter in iron skillet. Make a roux: add flour and brown lightly. Gradually add the water; stirring to blend. Add seasonings. Mix well. Add croutons and mix well to moisten. Combine with oyster mixture in skillet. Serve hot as a dip with small toasted bread squares or crackers. Also, makes a delicious dressing. Serves: 15

'O oysters,' said the Carpenter,
'You've had a pleasant run!
Shall we be trotting home again?'
But answer came there none –
And this was scarcely odd, because
They'd eaten every one.

TWEEDLEDEE
Lewis Carroll

Flight of Fancy Cheese Squares

10 eggs, beaten
1 teaspoon salt
1 teaspoon baking powder
½ cup flour, all-purpose
2 dashes Tabasco
2 cups cottage cheese, creamed
1 pound Monterey Jack cheese, shredded
½ cup butter, melted
2 4-ounce cans green chiles, chopped and seeded

Combine eggs with salt, baking powder, flour and Tabasco. Mix well. Add cheeses and butter; mix only to blend. Fold in green chiles. Pour into a buttered 9½ x 13 inch baking pan. Bake at 400 degrees for 15 minutes; then bake at 350 degrees for 35 minutes. Cut into bite-size squares. Serve hot. Yield: 24

"Many's the long night I've dreamed of cheese – toasted, mostly."
Robert Louis Stevenson, 1850-1894

Champion's Choice Eggplant Balls

1 large eggplant, peeled and cubed
1 egg, beaten
2 cups plain bread crumbs
3 tablespoons olive oil
salt

Boil cubed eggplant in salted boiling water for 8 minutes. Drain and remove excess water with paper towels. Mash thoroughly with fork. Combine mashed eggplant with egg and bread crumbs. Form into bite-size balls. Saute until brown in olive oil. Place on paper towels to absorb olive oil and quickly sprinkle with salt. Serve hot. Yield: 24

Mushroom Chandelle Rolls

1 loaf sandwich bread
1 onion, chopped
4 tablespoons butter
½ pound fresh mushrooms, chopped
¾ teaspoon thyme
½ teaspoon flour
¼ cup sour cream
salt and pepper to taste

Remove crust from bread and roll 24 slices paper thin. Saute onions in butter until golden. Add mushrooms. Cook about 5 minutes while stirring. Add thyme, flour, salt and pepper to taste and sour cream. Cook and stir until thickened. Place a tablespoon of mixture on each slice of bread. Roll like a jelly roll and place on cookie sheet with the edge side down. Brush with melted butter. Toast in oven until lightly browned at 450 degrees. Serve immediately. Yield: 24

Broccoli Cloud Puffs

2 10-ounce packages frozen, chopped broccoli
1 cup Bisquick baking mix
1 cup milk
2 eggs
½ teaspoon salt
1 cup sharp cheddar cheese, shredded

Prepare broccoli according to package directions; drain well.
Combine Bisquick, milk, eggs and salt. Beat with an electric
mixer until smooth. Stir in broccoli and cheese. Pour into a
buttered 1½ quart shallow baking dish. Bake at 325 degrees for
1 hour. Serves: 6 Serve hot or cold.
Alternate: Substitute 2 packages frozen corn or 2 packages
frozen chopped spinach.

Hot Prop Crab Dip

1 onion, chopped
3 tablespoons butter
1 tablespoon flour
1 can cream of tomato soup
1 large can crab meat
1 carton half and half
¼ cup dry sherry
¼ cup sharp cheese, grated

Saute onion in butter until tender, but do not brown. Add flour
and tomato soup while stirring. Cook on low heat until slightly
thickened. Add crab meat. Slowly add half and half. Heat
thoroughly. Remove from heat and add the sherry. Salt to taste.
Stir in cheese. Serve hot in pastry shells or with crackers.
Serves: 4

Picnic Pate

2 tablespoons butter
1 tablespoon corn oil
½ pound calf's liver, cut in 1 inch strips
½ pound mushroom caps
1 medium onion, sliced thinly
2 cloves garlic, pressed
1 tablespoon cognac
1 cup chicken bouillon
¼ teaspoon tarragon, crushed
¼ teaspoon dried dill weed
1 teaspoon salt
¼ teaspoon white pepper
1 tablespoon plain gelatin

Melt butter in a large heavy skillet and add the corn oil. Add the liver strips and saute until medium rare using medium heat (about 3 minutes on both sides). Remove the liver and set aside in a blender or food processor.

Combine mushroom caps, onion and garlic in skillet; add the cognac, cover and steam 5 minutes. Remove 10 caps and set aside.

Pour ¼ cup chicken bouillon over the liver in the blender and blend 1 minute on high. Add another ¼ cup chicken bouillon, the steamed mushroom mixture from the skillet, tarragon, dill, salt, and pepper; blend well on high.

Dissolve the gelatin in the remaining ½ cup of chicken bouillon. Add to liver mixture and blend well.

Pour ⅓ of the pate mixture into a glass bowl or compote mold (2½ cups). Place 5 mushroom caps, round-side down on top of the pate. Add another ⅓ cup of the pate and the remaining 5 mushroom caps on top. Pour and smooth the remaining pate over the caps. Chill 8 hours. The flavor will improve if left 24 hours. Unmold and serve with crackers or French bread slices. Serves: 6

"The best liver pate you will ever taste. The embedded caps make the pate slices most attractive."

Pickled GULF Shrimp

1 pound shrimp, cooked and peeled
2 tablespoons olive oil
1 cup vinegar
2 tablespoons water
¼ cup green onions, chopped
8 whole cloves
1 bay leaf
2 teaspoons salt
1 teaspoon sugar
dash Tabasco sauce
½ teaspoon garlic powder
½ teaspoon celery seed

Dribble oil over shrimp. Combine remaining ingredients and bring to a boil. Pour liquid over shrimp. Cover and refrigerate overnight. Serve chilled. Serves: 4

Smoked Salmon Tasty Crunchies

1 tablespoon minced dry onions
1 3-ounce cream cheese, soft
1 tablespoon mayonnaise
1 teaspoon lemon juice
¼ cup celery, diced
season to taste, thyme, salt, MSG
1 cup smoked salmon, flaked

Combine onions with cream cheese. Add remaining ingredients in order listed. Chill 2 hours. Serve as a spread on sandwiches or crackers. Yield: 1½ cups

Little Green Peppers Stuffed with Shrimp

3 tablespoons butter
½ cup onion, chopped finely
½ cup celery, chopped finely
1 teaspoon tomato paste
16 shrimp, peeled and deveined
¼ teaspoon salt
¼ teaspoon red pepper
¼ teaspoon white pepper
½ cup fine bread crumbs
8 little green peppers, cut in half and seeded

Melt butter in skillet; add onions, celery and tomato paste. Cook on medium heat until onions are clear. Add shrimp and cook about 6 minutes. Add seasonings. Remove from heat and gently stir in bread crumbs and mix well. Fill each little green pepper half with a shrimp and stuffing mix. Place in a baking dish and add topping below.

Topping:

1 tablespoon butter, melted
bread crumbs
1 8-ounce can tomato sauce

Brush tops of peppers lightly with melted butter and sprinkle with bread crumbs. Pour over tomato sauce and bake covered at 350 degrees for 15 minutes. Serves: 4 - 6. Yield: 16

"These are great little appetizers."

Supersonic Salmon Ball

2 cups canned salmon, drained and flaked
1 8-ounce package cream cheese, soft
1 teaspoon instant minced onion
1 tablespoon lemon juice
¼ teaspoon salt
1 teaspoon horseradish
¼ teaspoon liquid smoke
½ cup pecans, chopped
3 tablespoons parsley, chopped

Combine and mix all ingredients reserving pecans and parsley. Chill 4 hours, shape into a ball. Combine pecans and parsley. Roll ball in pecan and parsley mixture. Serve with crackers. Yield: 1 large ball

Swift Smoked Salmon Dip

1 8-ounce package cream cheese
⅓ cup sour cream
2 teaspoons horseradish
1 cup smoked salmon, flaked
¼ cup onion, chopped finely

Combine cream cheese, sour cream and horseradish; blend well. Add salmon and onion; mix well. Chill before serving as a dip with toasted bread squares or crackers. Yield: 2 cups

Alternate: After chilling 1 hour form a ball. Roll in finely chopped nuts or chopped parsely.

Caviar Mousse Aboard the GOOSE

1½ teaspoons gelatin, unflavored
2 tablespoons water, cold
4 ounces red lumpfish caviar, drained
1 8-ounce carton sour cream
¼ cup red onion, minced
¼ cup parsley, chopped
2 dashes red pepper
¾ cup whipping cream, whipped
watercress sprigs
cocktail rye bread

In a small bowl combine gelatin and water; soften 5 minutes. Stir to dissolve; set aside. Combine caviar, sour cream, onion, parsley and pepper in a medium mixing bowl; stir in gelatin mixture. Fold in whipped cream. Spoon into 3 cup mold. Chill covered until set (about 3 hours). To serve: unmold onto large platter lined with watercress sprigs. Serve with cocktail rye bread. Serves: Quite a Crew!

Camembert with Lingonberry Sauce

½ cup sauterne
¼ cup fresh lemon juice
2 cartons lingonberries, drained
1 cup sugar
2 teaspoons grated orange rind
1 tablespoon grated lemon rind
1 teaspoon ground cardamom
1 8-ounce round Camembert

Combine sauterne and lemon juice in a medium sauce pan. Cook on medium heat; reduce to about ¼ cup. Stir in lingonberries, sugar, rinds and cardamom. Bring to a boil; reduce to simmer until thickened (about 20 minutes). Stir occasionally. Cool. To serve: Place camembert on a large serving platter, spoon lingonberries and sauce around and over camembert. Serve with crackers. Serves: 8 - 12

Alternate: Forget the above, stir ½ teaspoon ground cardamom into 1 10-ounce jar wild lingonberries; heat and serve with Camembert.

See and Avoid Garlic

10 whole garlic pods
⅓ cup olive oil
1 cup chicken or beef broth
salt and pepper to taste

Peel away the outer skin of the garlic pods, but leave the individual cloves covered. Place in a shallow baking dish. Sprinkle with olive oil and pour over the broth. Season to taste. Bake at 350 degrees for 45 minutes; partially covered. Baste frequently. Remove cover last 10 minutes to brown skins. Serve with toasted bread squares or crackers. Also good with roasted chicken, beef or pork.

Variety's the very spice of life
That gives it all its flavour.

William Cooper, 1731-1800

Brie In a Cloud

6 sheets Phyllo pastry (12 x 17 inch)
1½ sticks butter, melted
1 whole Brie (about 2 pounds)
1 tablespoon prepared hot mustard
⅔ cup pecans, chopped
⅔ cup fig preserves

Layer 3 sheets of pastry and spread with butter. Layer 3 sheets of pastry in opposite direction to make a cross; spread with butter; set aside. Spread a thin layer of mustard over Brie. (Do Not Trim Brie.) Combine pecans and preserves to make a paste. Spread a thin layer of preserve mixture over mustard layer. Invert Brie and place in center of pastry. Overlap pastry to close, securing edges well. Brush top and sides with butter. Place Brie in a shallow pyrex dish to capture any leakage. Bake at 350 degrees for 30 minutes or until golden brown. Wait 30 - 45 minutes before serving. Serves: 4 - 6

"My most kind and lovable neighbor, Lucille Langenbeck"

BROILED GRAPEFRUIT

1 half grapefruit
1 to 1½ tablespoons butter
½ teaspoon sugar
2 tablespoons sugar-cinnamon mixture (1 part
    cinnamon to 4 parts sugar)
1 sauteed chicken liver

Take a room temperature grapefruit and cut every section of grapefruit half, close to the membrane. Cut a hole in the center of the grapefruit half and fill with 1 to 1½ tablespoons butter. Sprinkle ½ teaspoon sugar over each half, then sprinkle with 2 tablespoons cinnamon-sugar mixture. Broil grapefruit on a shallow baking pan or jelly roll pan 4 inches from heat for about 8 to 10 minutes or just long enough to brown tops. At the end of broiling time, place a chicken liver in center. Sprinkle lightly with sugar and broil about 2 minutes longer.

Chalet Suzanne
RESTAURANT
& COUNTRY INN

U. S. 27 North
LAKE WALES,
FLORIDA

Philip's Supper House
Scampi Appetizer

3 tablespoons flour
5 large jumbo shrimp, peeled and deveined
2 tablespoons oil
2 tablespoons butter
1 teaspoon pure lemon juice
1 tablespoon white wine
¼ teaspoon finely chopped fresh garlic
4 ounces whipping cream
½ teaspoon chopped parsley

Flour shrimp and place in hot skillet containing cooking oil. Turn shrimp frequently until golden brown. Drain off cooking oil and dispose. Add butter, lemon juice, wine, garlic and whipping cream while shrimp in skillet are still over low flame. Frequently shaking pan, turn flame a little higher until liquid reduces to thick sauce. Put on side dish, sprinkle with parsley. Serve hot.

4545 West Sahara Avenue
Las Vegas, Nevada 89102
(702) 873-5222

FLIGHT SNACKS

Captain Krunch

3 cups puffed -rice cereal
1 cup raisins
1 cup chopped dried apricots
1 cup dry-roasted unsalted peanuts
¼ cup flaked coconut
⅓ cup butter
1 package large marshmallows
½ cup peanut butter

Combine cereal, raisins, apricots, peanuts and coconut in large mixing bowl. In saucepan melt butter, marshmallows and peanut butter on low heat (covered). Stir until blended and smooth. Pour over cereal mixture and toss. Press gently into 13 x 9 inch baking dish and cut into squares. "Captain Krunch is a good traveler!"

So, munch on, crunch on,
take your nucheon,
Breakfast, supper, dinner,
luncheon!

THE PIED PIPER OF HAMELIN
Robert Browning, 1812-1889

Multi-Munch

2 quarts popped popcorn, unsalted
1 cup sunflower seeds
1 cup peanuts
2 tablespoons butter
¼ cup honey
1 tablespoon grated lemon peel
¼ teaspoon cinnamon

Prepare popcorn and place in large bowl with sunflower seeds and peanuts. Melt butter in saucepan; stir in honey, lemon peel and cinnamon. Drizzle over popcorn in large bowl and toss gently. Makes 2½ quarts and always ready to go!

Survival Snack

¼ cup cashew pieces
½ cup walnut pieces
2 cups raisins
¼ cup dried coconut
¾ cup chocolate chips

Toss together in a ziplock. "Always have some handy in your flight bag!"

Airborne Granola

1 cup wheat germ
1 cup soy flour
1 cup sesame seeds
1 cup slivered almonds
5 cups old-fashioned oats
1 cup shredded coconut
1 cup powdered milk
1 cup raisins
1 cup vegetable oil
1 cup honey

Combine dry ingredients in small garbage bag. Combine and stir vegetable oil and honey together. Combine with dry ingredients and gently toss. Spread mixture in large shallow baking pan. Bake at 250 degrees for 1 hour. Yield: 14 cups or about 10 ziplocks. An excellent snack with milk.

Flight Saver Snack

2 cups corn flakes
½ cup pretzel sticks
½ cup mixed nuts
1 cup angel flake coconut
½ teaspoon garlic salt
1 tablespoon butter, melted

Spread cereal in shallow baking pan. Toast in oven for 5 minutes at 325 degrees. Add remaining ingredients and mix well. Continue toasting 15 to 20 minutes, or until golden brown, stirring occasionally. Serve warm or cold. Yield: 3 small ziplocks, ON THE MOVE.

Tasty Pull Tubes, Rivets, Ball Joints, Nuts and Bolts

4 cups Crispix Cereal
2 cups Cheerios
2 cups Wheat Chex
2 packages (4.5 ounces) Sesame Sticks
2 cups mixed nuts
1 stick butter or margarine, melted
½ cup vegetable oil
2 teaspoons chili powder
2 teaspoons garlic salt
1 teaspoon seasoned salt
½ teaspoon onion salt
1 teaspoon accent
1 teaspoon cayenne pepper
2 tablespoons red hot sauce
1 tablespoon worcestershire sauce
¼ cup Parmesan cheese

Combine cereals, sesame sticks and nuts in a small garbage bag. Combine melted butter and vegetable oil with all seasonings. Pour over mixture in garbage bag and toss gently. Place in large shallow baking pan and bake 15 minutes at 250 degrees. Remove and sprinkle with cheese. Stir and return to oven and bake for 30 minutes stirring after 15 minutes. Cool on paper towels. Yield: Approximately 9 cups

Note: Use a liquid measure to measure the dry cereals.

"its cheerio
my deario that
pulls a lady through"

ARCHY and MEHITABEL
CHEERIO MY DEARIO
Donald Robert Marquis

AVIATION "HALL OF FAME"

SANDWICHES

and BUTTERS . . .

Cheese Notes for Sandwiches

American, Cheddar
All-around favorite for sandwiches or snacks.
Brick
Good for sandwiches. Combines well with fruit.
Cream Cheese
Excellent to add richness and body to sandwich spreads.
Edam, Gouda
Very good for sandwiches. Combines well with grapes and oranges.
Liederkranz, Limburger
A favorite used on pumpernickel or rye bread.
Mozzarella, Scamorze
Excellent for toasted sandwiches.
Muenster
A good choice for combination sandwiches.
Provolone
Good to use in Italian sandwiches.
Swiss
First choice for ham and cheese sandwiches.
Process Cheeses
Ideal for grilled cheese sandwiches.

Flightketeer Sandwich

8 slices Wright bread*
mayonnaise
2 cups alfalfa sprouts or 4 leaves Romaine lettuce
1 large ripe avocado, sliced ¼ inch thick (4 slices)
8 ounces muenster cheese, grated
salt to taste

Spread bread slices with mayonnaise. On each slice place a layer of alfalfa or one leaf of romaine lettuce. Place the four slices of avocado on top of 4 alfalfa covered bread slices. Cover avocado slices with cheese. Cover and close sandwiches with alfalfa covered bread slices. Cut as desired for easy handling and eating. Yield: 4 uncut sandwiches

*(See index)

*There is no love sincerer than
the love of food.*

TANNER
George Bernard Shaw, 1856-1950

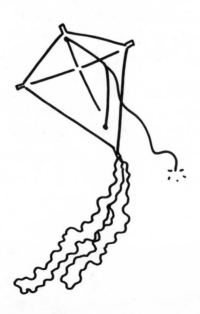

The Whirley-Bird Sandwich

3 tablespoons mayonnaise
1 tablespoon horseradish
1 tablespoon creole mustard
8 slices French bread
1 cup Crew Cut Cabbage Slaw*
4 slices Swiss cheese
4 slices cooked roast beef
4 slices tomato

Blend mayonnaise,horseradish and mustard; spread evenly on each bread slice. Equally top 4 bread slices with slaw, cheese, roast beef and tomato. Top with remaining bread slices; mixture side down. Slice as desired. Yield: 4 sandwiches

*(See index)

Olive Nut Butter

1 8-ounce cream cheese, soft
½ cup mayonnaise
½ cup pecans, chopped finely
1 cup salad olives, chopped
2 tablespoons olive juice
dash black pepper

Mash the cream cheese with a fork to blend mayonnaise. Stir in pecans, salad olives, juice and pepper; mix well. Chill before serving. Spread on sandwich bread or toast topped with lettuce leaves. Yield: 1 pint.

Sweet Fruit Butters

Strawberry:

> 1 stick unsalted butter, soft
> ½ cup strawberry preserves
> 1 teaspoon fresh lemon juice
> ½ teaspoon powdered sugar

Combine and blend ingredients. Spread into a small crock and refrigerate to firm. Will keep several days in refrigerator and freezes well. Serve at room temperature. Yield: 1 cup "Sweet butters are wonderful for a picnic with tea cakes or just plain toast."

Red currant:

> ¾ cup cream cheese
> 1 tablespoon cream
> 1 teaspoon powdered sugar
> 3 tablespoons red currant preserves

Combine cream cheese and cream to make a paste. Add and blend other ingredients. Chill in small crock, but serve at room temperature. "Delicious on waffles or pancakes."

The "Chuck" Yaeger

1 8-ounce cream cheese, soft
2 tablespoons milk
2 tablespoons mayonnaise
1 12-ounce can corned beef
½ cup green onion, chopped
2 teaspoons horseradish
2 teaspoons prepared mustard
8 slices white or brown bread

Combine cream cheese with milk and mayonnaise with a fork to blend. Add corned beef, onions, horseradish and mustard. Blend well. Spread on choice of bread and broil 10 minutes. Serve hot open-faced. This mixture is great for canapes or cracker spread. Serves: 4

The WRIGHT Sandwich

2 tablespoons cranberry sauce
4 slices French bread (1 inch thick)
2 slices Muenster cheese
2 slices cooked turkey
4 tablespoons butter, soft

Spread sauce evenly on each bread slice. Equally top 2 bread slices with cheese and turkey; top with remaining bread cranberry sauce side down. Spread 2 tablespoons butter equally on outside of bread slices. In a medium skillet, melt remaining butter. Cook sandwiches, covered, on medium heat until cheese is melted and sandwiches are golden brown (about 15 minutes). Turn only once. Press down sandwiches with spatula occasionally. Yield: 2

The BIG Sandwich Loaf

1 3-ounce cream cheese, soft
1 8-ounce can crushed pineapple, drained
1 large loaf white or whole wheat bread, whole
1 recipe Lemon-Curry Butter*
3 tablespoons watercress, whole
1 recipe Chicken Salad*
9 lettuce leaves

Combine the cream cheese with pineapple and mix well; set aside. Trim the crusts from both ends of the loaf. Cut the loaf into 3 or 4 lengthwise slices. Spread the inner sides of the slices with lemon-curry butter. Layer watercress on buttered slices. Spread a layer of chicken salad. Spread a layer of the pineapple mixture. Layer lettuce leaves. Place top slice over lettuce to close sandwich. Wrap in a moist kitchen cloth and clear plastic wrap. Refrigerate 3 hours. Holds well. When ready to serve, sandwiches may be sliced to desired thickness. "A delightful charmer." Serves: 6 - 8

*(See index)

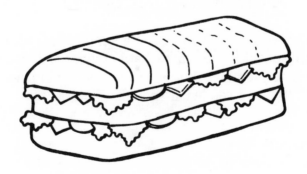

Mini DOG-LEG Sandwiches

2 tablespoons butter, soft
2 tablespoons creole mustard
8 slices white bread
1 cup Crew Cut Cabbage Slaw*
4 slices Swiss cheese
4 slices cooked ham
4 slices tomato

Blend butter with mustard; spread evenly on each bread slice. Equally top 4 bread slices with slaw, cheese, ham and tomato. Top with remaining bread, buttered side down.   Cut each sandwich into triangles. Yield: 16 mini sandwiches

*(See index)

Lemon-Curry Butter

½ cup butter, soft
1 teaspoon lemon juice
¼ teaspoon lemon rind
½ teaspoon curry powder
2 tablespoons chives, chopped

Gradually combine soft butter with lemon juice. Beat in lemon rind, curry powder and chives until creamy and smooth. Chill butter firm and form into butter curls or balls, mold in a small clay crock, or use as a sandwich spread. Yield: ½ pint

Spinach Salad in a Roll

8-inch long French Roll
spinach, washed and dry
4 teaspoons vinaigrette dressing*
2 boiled eggs, sliced
3 slices bacon, fried
salt and pepper to taste

Split roll in half, but not quite through. Scoop out some of center to make room for filling. Line bottom of roll with spinach, drizzle with 2 teaspoons vinaigrette dressing. Pile on slices of cooked crisp bacon. Top bacon with hard-boiled egg slices. Add salt and pepper to taste and cover with layer of spinach drizzled with 2 teaspoons dressing. Add roll top. Secure with tooth pick.
Serves: 2

*(See index)

The Hungary Airwolf

1½ pints sour cream
½ cup prepared mustard
4 tablespoons parsley, chopped
½ teaspoon black pepper
2 teaspoons salt
3 tablespoons onion flakes
1 loaf French bread (6 feet long)
2 pounds sliced cooked turkey
2 pounds sliced cooked roast beef
1½ pounds sliced Swiss cheese
4 large tomatoes, sliced
2 large avocados, sliced
lettuce, shredded

In a medium bowl, blend first 6 ingredients; chill. Cut bread in half horizontally. Spread chilled mixture on each bread half. On bottom bread half, layer turkey, roast beef, cheese, tomatoes, avocados and lettuce. Top with the remaining bread slice. Serves: 20

PICKLIN' 'N PRESERVIN'

STANDARD CERTIFIED BASIC PICNIC CHECKLIST:

parachute tablecloth
picnic basket
vacuum containers
thermos for hot liquids
thermos for cold liquids
insulated flight bag for ice or cold beverages
aluminum foil
zip lock bags
flatware, plates, glasses or cups
can and bottle opener
small tray with shallow edges/cutting board
towelettes
paper towels, napkins
sharp knife
garbage bag with tie
serving spoon

If leaving aircraft remove:
flashlight/matches
first aid kit with sunscreen and insect repellant

Precise Strawberry Jam

3½ pounds fresh strawberries
3 tablespoons lemon juice
3 pounds sugar

Hull the strawberries and use a damp kitchen cloth to clean away the dirt. Place berries in a deep heavy saucepan or preserving pan with the lemon juice. On medium heat cook the berries gently until soft; stirring gently (about 30 minutes). Add the sugar and stir to dissolve. Increase heat and bring to a boil. Do not stir. Boil hard until the setting point is reached, 105 degrees Celsius or 221 degrees Fahrenheit. Skim the top to remove any surface scum. Let stand 15 - 20 minutes. Pour into clean warm jars and seal while hot. Yield: 5 pints

"A modification of a recipe from Grandmother Qualls."

Curly locks, Curly locks,
wilt thou be mine?
Thou shalt not wash dishes
nor yet feed the swine,
But sit on a cushion
and sew a fine seam,
And feed upon strawberries,
Sugar and cream.

Infant Institutes, 1797

Pickled Sweet Okra

3 pounds fresh okra, young small pods
6 teaspoons dill seed
6 teaspoons celery seed
6 garlic cloves
6 pods hot pepper, optional
1 cup sugar
½ cup salt, plain
1 quart water
1 quart white vinegar

Wash and drain okra. Pack into 6 pint jars. Divide dill seed, celery seed, cloves and hot pepper equally among the jars. Combine sugar, salt, water and vinegar in a large saucepan. Bring to a boil; boil 1 minute. Pour into jars to within ½ inch of top. Seal jars and place in hot water bath for 8 minutes. Cool.
Yield: 6 pints

Rhubarb Jam

3 pounds rhubarb
3 pounds sugar
4 tablespoons fresh lemon juice
grated rind of 2 lemons
1 teaspoon all spice

Wash the rhubarb, drain and cut into small chunks. Layer in a nonmetal covered container with the sugar and lemon juice. Let stand covered 8 hours. Place rhubarb mixture and lemon rind into a preserving pan. Bring slowly to a boil; stirring to dissolve the sugar. Continue to boil until the mixture is transparent and reaches 221 degrees (about 30 minutes). Remove any surface scum and pour into warm, sterile jars. Yield: 5 pints

Apple Mint Jet Jel

3 pounds green skinned cooking apples
2¼ pints water, approximately
1 bunch fresh mint
juice of 2 lemons
sugar
green food coloring
3 tablespoons fresh mint, chopped finely

Wash the apples, chop roughly (without removing peel or cores) and put into a heavy pot with the water, mint and lemon juice. Bring to a boil and simmer until soft and pulpy. Mash well and strain through a jelly bag or cloth. Measure juice and place in a preserving pan with 1 pound of sugar to each 1 pint of juice. Heat gently until the sugar is dissolved; stirring frequently. Bring to a boil; boil 5 minutes. Add the chopped mint and continue to boil until setting point (105 degrees celsius or 221 degrees farenheit). Remove any foam from the surface and add green coloring if desired. Let stand until a thin skin forms on the surface. This helps to keep the chopped mint evenly distributed through the set jelly. Pour into small warmed jars. Cool, label and store in a cool, dark place. Yield: 4 pints

Pineapple Pickles

1½ cups pineapple juice, canned
1¼ cups white vinegar
¾ cups sugar
1 stick cinnamon
1 tablespoon whole cloves
½ teaspoon salt
1 large pineapple, peeled and cut in chunks

In a medium sauce pan bring the pineapple juice, vinegar, sugar, cinnamon, cloves and salt to a boil; stir to dissolve sugar. Boil 10 minutes. Add pineapple and simmer uncovered until the pineapple is clear and transparent (45 minutes to 1 hour). Yield: 1 pint. Serve as a condiment, garnish or topping for ice cream.

Crab An Apple Pickle

1 gallon crab apples
30 whole cloves
1 stick cinnamon
1 tablespoon whole all spice
1 tablespoon ginger
3 cups water
4 cups cider vinegar
8 cups sugar

Wash the apples well and pierce with a needle syringe. Tie the spices in cheesecloth. In a large container, heat the liquids, sugar and spices; stir to dissolve the sugar. Cool. Add the apples and simmer until tender. Cool, cover and let stand overnight. Place apples in hot, clean jars. Let the syrup boil 1 minute and pour over apples. Process jars in hot bath for 5 minutes. Yield: 5 pints

Loads of Vegetable Pickles

6 white turnips
2½ cups water
2 small beets, halved
1½ cups white vinegar
2½ teaspoons salt
4 garlic cloves, minced

Clean turnips well and cut a thin slice from top and bottom (do not peel). Cut each turnip into 3 inch strips. Cover with water and soak overnight. Rinse and drain; place in a glass container; add beets, vinegar, salt and garlic. Cover and rest at room temperature for 3 days. Serve chilled or room temperature. Yield: 2 pints

Alternate choices: cauliflower, carrots, cucumber, eggplant and celery.

Damson Preserves

1 gallon Damsons, ripe
water
1 pound sugar per 1 pound pulp

Destem and clean damsons. Squeeze gently to remove seeds; reserve seeds. Cut fruit into small pieces and place in large heavy pot. Cover with water and cook until fruit is tender. Pass cooked fruit through a strainer and weigh pulp. (Weigh container first and then deduct container weight.) Return pulp to heavy skillet and add 1 pound sugar per 1 pound pulp. Cover the reserved seeds with water; bring to a boil. Continue to cook to soft ball stage. Pour water from seeds over pulp in skillet. Cook slowly to a boil. Remove any top foam. Cook until thick. Pour into sterile jars and seal. Yield: 4 pints

"This fruit is ripe and ready for harvest in late August and September. Aunt Bea makes the best and this is her recipe!"

Airworthy Apple Butter

4 pounds Winesap apples, about 10 medium
1 cup water
1 cup cider vinegar
sugar
1 tablespoon cinnamon
1 teaspoon cloves
½ teaspoon all spice

Wash apples, remove stems and quarter. Place apples in a large heavy pot with water and vinegar; cook on medium low heat uncovered until soft. Press through a strainer, measure pulp and return to pot. Add ½ cup sugar to each cup of pulp. Add seasonings. Stir well to dissolve sugar. Continue cooking on medium low heat; stirring frequently until the mixture reaches 220 degrees fahrenheit (about 30 minutes). Ladle into hot sterilized jars. Yield: 3 pints

"Label and store in a dark pantry until your next picnic."

BEVERAGES

*"Up above the world you fly,
Like a tea-tray in the sky."*

ALICE'S ADVENTURES IN WONDERLAND

Lewis Carroll

Chocolate Carburetor Heat

½ cup water
2½ unsweetened chocolate squares,
    cut in pieces
¾ cup sugar
1 dash salt
½ cup whipping cream, whipped
6 cups hot milk

In saucepan cook water and chocolate on low heat until the chocolate is melted and blended (about 4 minutes). Stir in sugar and salt; continue to cook about 4 more minutes until smooth and thick. Cool. Prepare whipped cream and fold into chocolate mixture. To serve place two heaping tablespoons of mixture in a cup or mug. Fill with hot milk and stir with cinnamon or peppermint stick. Serves: 6

"A storm in a Teacup."

William Bayle Bernard

Irish Coffee Thrust

2 ounces whiskey
1 teaspoon brown sugar
1 cup strong coffee
3 tablespoons whipped cream

Combine the whiskey and sugar in a heatproof glass and mix well. Prepare whipped cream by whipping only enough to form soft peaks and soft enough to trickle off a spoon. Pour in the coffee. Add whipping cream by letting it gently trickle off the back of a tablespoon. Do not stir. It is better to make these one at a time.

"We'll take a cup o' Kindness yet,
For auld lang syne."

Robert Burns

Old Fashioned Picnic Lemonade

¾ cup sugar
1 cup lukewarm water
1 dozen lemons
lemon rinds, cut in strips
1 lemon for garnish, sliced
ice cubes
crushed ice

Dissolve the sugar in lukewarm water and add the juice of 1 dozen lemons. Mix and pour into 1 quart size thermos. Toss in the lemon rinds and fill with ice cubes. When ready to serve, pour over ¾ cup crushed ice and garnish with lemon slice.
Serves: 6 - 8

"When fate hands us a lemon,
let's try to make a lemonade."

Dale Carnegie

Cherry Rivet Bounce

2 quarts cherries, stemmed and cleaned
3 cups sugar
1 quart good bourbon

Place cleaned cherries in a large crock. Cover with sugar and mix gently. Cover the crock with a kitchen cloth and rest the cherries 12 - 14 days. Be sure to stir gently every other day. Stir in the bourbon. Recover with kitchen cloth and rest 24 hours. Strain through a kitchen cloth and pour into bottles.

"Place in reserve section with your 'private label'."

Cabin Coffee Float

3 cups cold water
6 squares sweet chocolate, cut-up
½ cup coffee, regular grind
orange peel strips
Whipped topping
grated chocolate

Using a 6 or 8 cup percolator; pour in water and add chocolate pieces. Place coffee and orange strips in basket or liner. Percolate gently 7 minutes on medium high. Remove from heat and remove basket. Serve hot with whipped topping and grated chocolate for garnish. Makes 3 cups or 7 demitasse.

> *"Look here, Steward, if this is
> coffee I want tea; but if this
> is tea, then I wish for coffee."*
>
> PUNCH   Vol. 123, 44   1902

Pilot's Punch

2 cups fresh orange juice
⅔ cup fresh lemon juice
½ cup sugar
2 teaspoons almond extract
1 32 ounce bottle cranberry juice cocktail
1 46 ounce can unsweetened pineapple juice
1 33.8 ounce bottle ginger ale, chilled

Combine all ingredients except the ginger ale and chill. To serve stir in the ginger ale mixing well. Yield: 4 quarts

"Let's have a hanger party in August."

> *"Old friends and old wine are best"*
> OUTLANDISH PROVERBS, Herbert 1640

Turbocharger

4 cups fresh vegetables, any combination of:
    spinach, lettuce, squash, celery, carrot or
    broccoli
3 cups water
10 fresh ripe tomatoes, unpeeled
3 chicken bouillon cubes
2 onions, chopped
1 whole garlic bud, separated
3 bay leaves
½ teaspoon salt
1 teaspoon dried basil

Place vegetables in large stockpot. Add two cups water. Place tomatoes in blender. Dissolve chicken cubes in remaining cup of water and add to tomatoes in blender. Liquefy the tomatoes and add to the vegetables in stockpot. Add chopped onions, garlic, bay leaves, salt and basil to stockpot. Bring to a boil for 20 minutes. Cover and allow to cool slightly. Remove bay leaves and strain through a colander or sieve. Serve hot or cold. Keep refrigerated. Yield: 6 servings. A good Bloody Mary Mix.

"An excellent nourishing hot or cold beverage to help maintain strength and stamina."

*Now stir the fire, and close the
shutters fast, Let fall the curtain,
wheel the sofa round, And
while the bubbling and loud –
hissing urn Throws up a
steamy column, and the cups,
That cheer but not inebriate,
wait on each, so let us
welcome peaceful evening in.*

William Cowper
1731 - 1800

Clear Ice Ring

"Clear ice can be fun if floating on a favorite punch!"

Select a ring mold which will fit into your punch bowl. Fill the mold with distilled water or tap water allowing space for expansion and decorative garnish. If you use tap water, let stand to eliminate air bubbles (2 - 3 hours). Float combinations of flowers and greenery on top and freeze. Place a moist hot kitchen cloth around mold to remove the Clear Ice Ring.

Party Prop Wash

3 cups sugar
3 cups water
1 No. 2 can grapefruit sections
1 No. 2 can crushed pineapple
juice of ½ lemon
1 16 ounce bottle 7up or ginger ale
maraschino cherries for garnish

Mix sugar and water to dissolve. Cut-up grapefruit sections into small pieces (or chop in blender). Add grapefruit sections with juice to sugar mixture; add crushed pineapple with juice to sugar mixture. Mix well and stir in the lemon juice. Pour into 3 ice cube trays and freeze to make fruit ice cubes. To serve fill cocktail glass with fruit ice cubes and fill with 7up or ginger ale. Garnish with cherry. Serves: 4

"It was a miracle of rare device,
a sunny pleasure-dome with caves of ice!"

KUBLA KHAN
Samuel Taylor Coleridge, 1772 - 1834

YEAST
BREADS

"Delightful Risings"

SHAPING ROLLS

Be Creative!

*"Take an object. Do something
to it. Do something else to it"*

Jasper Jones

Butterflake or Fan Rolls

Roll dough into a thin rectangular sheet.
Brush with melted butter and cut into strips about
1½ inches wide. Place 5, 6, or 7 strips on top of
each other. Cut strips ½ inches long and place
end down in muffin pans. Allow to rise before
baking.

Cloverleaf

Form dough into balls about the size of large
marbles. Dip balls into melted butter. Place
three balls touching each other in greased cup of
muffin tin. Allow to rise before baking.

Crescent

Divide dough into three equal parts and roll
into a circle 10 - 12 inches in diameter. Cut each
circle into pie-shaped pieces. Beginning with the
larger end, roll each pie-shaped piece sealing the
small end. Place on baking sheet 2 inches apart
with the point of the dough underneath. Form a
crescent shape by curving each piece. (Allow to
rise. Then, brush with melted butter.)

Parker House Rolls

Roll out dough to ½ inch thickness. Cut out
with biscuit cutter. Crease each biscuit with the
dull edge of a knife a little off center. After
brushing with melted butter, fold the large side
over the small side. Seal edges. Place on greased
baking sheet 1 inch apart. Allow to rise double in
bulk. Brush top with melted butter.

Pan Rolls

Form dough into balls about ⅓ the size of a
desired baked roll. Place balls in shallow baking
pan about ¼ inch apart. Allow to rise until double
in bulk. Brush with melted butter.

Ultra Lite Ice Box Rolls

2 packages dry yeast
¼ cup lukewarm water (Not Hot)
¾ cup sugar
2 teaspoons salt
1 cup solid vegetable shortening
1 cup boiling water
2 eggs
7 cups flour, all-purpose

Dissolve yeast in lukewarm water, set aside. Combine sugar, salt and shortening. Blend and mix well. Add boiling water and stir until blended. Add yeast mixture and mix. Add eggs and all the flour and mix well. Place in refrigerator overnight. Remove and roll out 2 hours before baking. Use biscuit cutter to cut out and brush with melted butter. Bake at 450 degrees for 15 - 20 minutes. Yield: 6 dozen rolls

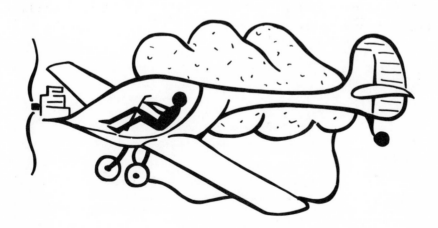

Four Point Rolls

1 package dry yeast
¼ cup warm water
4¾ cups flour, all-purpose sifted
1 cup butter
2 eggs, beaten
1 cup milk, scalded and cooled
¼ cup sugar
½ teaspoon salt
1 cup parmesan cheese
5½ tablespoons butter, melted

Dissolve yeast in water. In large bowl combine 3 cups flour, eggs, milk, sugar, salt and yeast. Blend and gradually add remaining flour to form dough. Cover and chill dough 2 - 3 hours (may be refrigerated up to 4 days to accommodate your flying schedule). Divide dough into 4 parts, roll out one part on floured surface to a 10" circle. Brush with 1 tablespoon butter and sprinkle with 3 tablespoons cheese. Cut into 8 wedges (like a pie). Roll each wedge, starting with the wide end and rolling each to the point. Form into crescent shape. Place on a buttered baking sheet. Repeat with remaining 3 portions. Let rise in a warm place until doubled in size (about 1 hour). Bake 15 - 18 minutes at 375 degrees. Yield: 40 rolls

Snap Rolls

1 cup warm water
½ cup milk, scalded and cooled
2 packages dry yeast
5 cups flour, all-purpose
1½ tablespoons sugar
2 teaspoons salt
3 tablespoons shortening

Dissolve yeast in warm water and add milk. Combine 2½ cups flour, salt and sugar in large bowl. Cut in shortening. Add yeast mixture and beat and knead until smooth. Add remaining flour and work to a firm dough (should be easily handled without sticking). Roll out dough to ¼ inch thickness on a lightly-floured board and cut into rounds with a biscuit cutter. Dip one half of each roll in melted butter and fold over other half, extending the top beyond the bottom. Place on a baking sheet close together. Cover with a kitchen cloth and let stand in a warm place until double in bulk (about 30 minutes). Bake for 15 - 20 minutes at 350 degrees. Yield: 3 dozen rolls

Brunch Bread

3 tablespoons sugar
3 eggs
1 stick butter (soft)
¼ teaspoon salt
2 cups flour, all-purpose
2 packages dry yeast
3 tablespoons water (lukewarm)

Beat eggs and sugar until light and fluffy. Add soft butter, salt and flour. Dissolve yeast in water and add. Beat well for three minutes. Place in greased loaf pan. Allow to rise in warm place until double bulk (about 2 hours). Bake at 400 degrees for 20 minutes. Yield: 1 loaf

Homemade Yeast Rolls

Dissolve 2 packages yeast in
¼ cup (warm, not hot) water with
2 tablespoons sugar. Set aside

In 2 cups milk, melt 1 stick margarine and 1 tablespoon salt.
Simmer until small bubbles form at edge of saucepan. Remove
from heat and let cool to warm temperature.

In large mixing bowl, measure 6 cups High Gluten or Bread
Flour. Pour yeast mixture into milk mixture; mix, then pour into
large bowl with the flour. Mix well until all ingredients are
absorbed into flour. Cover with a damp towel. Allow to rise until
double, or fingers pressed in dough leave an imprint. Knead on
floured pastry cloth for 15 - 20 minutes. Make out rolls. Allow to
rise until double in size. Bake 425 degrees for 8 - 10 minutes.
Enjoy!

Marilyn Chandler

635 Highway 98E
Destin, Florida

Note: This is a cozy place to eat, and the food is delicious!
    (About 5 minutes from Miracle Strip Airport in Destin.)

Home Built Yeast Rolls

1 quart milk
1 cup solid shortening
½ cup sugar
2 packages dry yeast
1 tablespoon salt
1½ teaspoons baking powder
1 teaspoon soda
8 cups flour, all-purpose

In saucepan combine first three ingredients and heat until shortening and sugar are melted. Cool. Add yeast and sift in 4 cups flour. Mix to make a cake-like batter. Let rise in a warm place. Dough should double in size within 30 minutes to an hour. Combine salt, soda and baking powder and add along with four more cups flour. Work in until dough is stiff and smooth. Place in large bowl and put in refrigerator covered until ready to use. Remove dough two hours before ready to bake. Roll out on floured surface to one-half inch thickness. Cut out with biscuit cutter, brush with melted butter and fold over half-way. Place in baking pan about one-half inch apart. Brush tops with butter. Cover with a clean dish cloth and let rise in a warm place (between one and two hours). Bake rolls as soon as they are ready at 400 degrees until brown (about 8 - 10 minutes).
Yield: 6 dozen rolls

The Wright Wheat Bread

2 packages active dry yeast
4 cups warm water
¼ cup vegetable oil
½ cup honey (from local bees is possible)
10¼ cups whole wheat flour
1¼ cups unprocessed bran
1½ teaspoons salt

Place yeast in large bowl. Gradually add 2 cups warm water. Gradually add 2 more cups warm water. Add oil and honey and stir. Add flour all at once with the bran and salt. Mix with a large spoon until all the liquid is staturated. Remove spoon and continue to blend ingredients with hands. Knead until the dough is not sticky. Add a little more flour if necessary. Lightly coat dough with vegetable oil on bottom and top and place back in the large bowl. Cover with light kitchen cloth or cheese cloth and place in a warm place without a draft. The dough should double in bulk in about two hours. Punch dough down and place on a lightly greased dough board. Knead for 1 minute and divide into 2 equal parts. Toss each part against the dough board 3 times. Form each part into a loaf and place into lightly greased loaf pan, press gently. Run a kitchen knife tip down the center of each loaf. Cover with kitchen cloth and let rise 30 minutes in a warm place. Preheat oven to 350 degrees and bake loaves for 1 hour and 10 minutes. Remove from pans immediately and wrap in kitchen towels and plastic wrap until cooled. Rewrap in plastic and refrigerate or freeze. Yield: 2 large loaves

Note: This is my favorite bread for toast or sandwiches. It also makes a lovely gift simply wrapped in plastic with ribbon.

The King asked
The Queen, and
The Queen asked
The Dairymaid:
'Could we have some butter for
The Royal slice of bread?'

THE KING'S BREAKFAST
A. A. Milne

Lighter-Than-Air Sour Dough Rolls

1 package dry yeast
¼ cup water, lukewarm
1 cup sour dough starter, See below
3 tablespoons vegetable oil
2¼ cups self-rising flour

Combine yeast and warm water to dissolve. Combine with remaining ingredients to make a soft dough. Knead 2 - 3 minutes. Place in warm place and allow to rise about 1 hour. Punch down dough and form into a loaf. Place in greased loaf pan and let rise again in warm place (about 30 minutes). Bake at 400 degrees for 15 minutes. Yield: 1 regular size loaf (or 1 dozen clover leaf rolls, or 2½ dozen cocktail or mini clover leaf rolls).

Sour dough starter:

2 cups flour, all-purpose
2 cups milk
½ cup sugar

Combine ingredients in covered container. Place in refrigerator. The starter will be ready to use after resting three days. The starter will keep for two weeks or more while refrigerated. The starter should be fed every five to seven days or as you use it. To feed starter simply add the original ingredients in the same quantities.

"A favorite family recipe from Aunt Bea!"

Delicious Dutch Rolls

2 packages dry yeast
1 cup milk, lukewarm
1 teaspoon salt
2 tablespoons sugar
Dash nutmeg
3 eggs
3 tablespoons butter, melted and cooled
6 cups flour, all-purpose

Dissolve yeast in milk in large mixing bowl. Add all other ingredients except flour. Mix and blend well. Gradually stir in the flour and mix well. Cover with kitchen cloth and let rise until double in bulk (about 2 hours). Knead down and remove two pieces at a time (the size of eggs) and place in buttered muffin tins. Bake for 15 - 20 minutes at 375 degrees. Yield: 6 dozen rolls

QUICK BREADS

THIS IS YOUR CAPTAIN SPEAKING

"A few friendly reminders:"

Don't forget to preheat your engines, UH! ovens unless otherwise directed.

Don't bother to sift flour or other ingredients unless otherwise directed. Simply level off with a sharp edge; or if in a hurry, shake off the excess and keep on going.

Do untighten your seatbelt and shoulder harness, and get ready for smooth flying, good food and fun.

THE FLYING GOURMET
Squaking 1200
Good Day

Lofty Cheese Loaf

1 cup cornmeal (yellow)
1 cup flour, all-purpose
¼ cup sugar
1 tablespoon baking powder
2 teaspoons caraway seeds
1 teaspoon seasoned salt
2 eggs, beaten
1⅓ cup milk
6 ounces cheddar cheese, grated

Combine cornmeal, flour, sugar, baking powder, caraway seeds and seasoned salt. Mix and blend well. Add the beaten eggs, milk and grated cheese. Stir well to blend. Pour into 9 inch greased and floured loaf pan. Bake at 400 degrees for 35 minutes. Remove immediately from pan and cool on wire rack. Delicious! Yield: 1 loaf or 3 small loaves

*The lion and the Unicorn
    were fighting for the Crown;
The lion beat the unicorn
    all around the town.*

*Some gave them white Bread,
    and some gave them brown;
Some gave them plum cake
    And drummed them out of
    town.*

WILLIAM KING

Fly to New Orleans for Oyster Bread

1 cup milk
1 cup heavy cream
1 cup yellow cornmeal
¼ cup Parmesan cheese
2½ tablespoons melted butter
1 10½-ounce can cream of celery soup, undiluted
1 tablespoon flour
1 teaspoon baking powder
½ teaspon herb seasoning
1 teaspoon salt
3 eggs, separated
1 dozen fresh oysters, drained and cut in half
1 4-ounce can mushroom slices
paprika

In skillet combine milk, cream and cornmeal; bring to a boil 2 minutes; remove from heat. Add cheese, butter and soup. Sift flour, baking powder, herb seasoning and salt; beat into cornmeal mixture. Beat egg yolks well and stir in with oysters and mushrooms. Beat the egg whites stiff and fold into the mixture. Pour into a well-greased 2 quart casserole dish; sprinkle with paprika. Bake at 325 degrees for 1 hour. Yield: 6 servings

Inverted Vegetable Bread

½ cup onion, chopped
1 16-ounce package frozen mixed vegetables
1 8½-ounce package corn muffin mix
½ teaspoon dried parsley
salt and pepper to taste

Cook vegetables as directed on package with the onion. Drain in colander. Spread into a buttered 8 inch square pan. Prepare corn muffin mix as directed on package; stir in caraway seed. Spoon over vegetables. Bake at 400 degrees for 25 minutes. Cut into squares. Yield: 6 servings

"Interesting and good"

Timed Turn Popovers

1¼ cups milk
1¼ cups flour, all-purpose
½ teaspoon salt
3 eggs

Combine the milk, flour and salt in medium mixing bowl. Mix well with wire whisk. Add eggs one at a time and mix until just blended. Pour into greased popover cups. Bake at 450 degrees for 20 minutes and then bake at 350 for 15 - 20 minutes until brown. Serve hot. Yield: 6 popovers

Hot Air Balloon Puffs

1 cup sugar
5 tablespoons shortening
1 egg, separated
1½ cups all-purpose flour, sifted
¼ teaspoon salt
2¼ teaspoon baking powder
¼ teaspoon nutmeg
½ cup milk
6 tablespoons melted butter
½ teaspoon cinnamon

Gradually add ½ cup sugar to shortening and cream until fluffy. Stir in the egg yolk. Sift together the flour, salt, baking powder and nutmeg; add to shortening alternately with the milk. Beat the egg white stiff and fold in batter mixture. Line muffin tins with paper cups and fill ¾ full. Bake at 350 degrees for 20 - 25 minutes. While puffs are baking prepare ½ cup sugar and cinnamon. In separate bowl prepare melted butter. Dip baked hot air balloon puffs into melted butter then sugar-cinnamon mixture. Serve hot. Yield: 12

Easy to do and fun to eat!

Regal Eagle Beer Bread

3 cups self-rising flour
¼ cup sugar
12 ounces beer
melted butter

Mix flour, sugar and beer until blended. Place in greased 9 x 5 x 3 inch loaf pan. Bake at 375 degrees for 1 hour. Drizzle with butter. Serve hot. Yield: 1 loaf

Fly-Off-the-Plate Waffles

2 cups flour, all-purpose
3 teaspoons baking powder
½ teaspoon salt
2 tablespoons sugar
3 eggs, separated
1¾ cups milk
½ cup butter, melted

Sift flour; measure and resift with dry ingredients. Beat egg yolks and combine with milk and melted butter. Pour into dry ingredients and beat until smooth. Beat egg whites stiff and fold into batter gently but thoroughly. Bake in medium-hot waffle iron until golden brown. (About 3 minutes) For special waffles, sprinkle 2 tablespoons chopped nuts over waffle before baking. Serve with maple syrup. Yield: 8 - 10 waffles

"A little of what you fancy does you good."

Marie Lloyd
1870-1922

Rectangular Coarse Corn Bread

1 stick butter
1 cup flour, all-purpose
1¼ cups yellow corn meal
4 teaspoons baking powder
1 teaspoon salt
2 tablespoons sugar
¾ cup milk
1 egg

Melt butter in 12 x 8 inch baking pan in oven at 425 degrees. In a medium mixing bowl combine all the dry ingredients. Stir to blend dry ingredients. Beat the egg and milk together and pour over cornmeal mixture. Pour the hot melted butter over the egg mixture. Stir only enough to blend. Pour into hot baking pan. Bake for 30 minutes at 425 degrees. Serves: 6

Magnetic Compliments Corn Bread

¾ cup corn meal (yellow)
1 cup flour, all-purpose
⅓ cup sugar
¾ teaspoon salt
1 teaspoon baking soda
2 teaspoons cream of tartar
1 cup sour cream
¼ cup milk
1 egg, beaten
2 tablespoons butter, melted

Mix and sift together all the dry ingredients. Mix the sour cream with the milk, and add to dry ingredients with the egg and melted butter. Pour into buttered 8 inch square baking pan. Bake at 425 degrees for 20 minutes. Yield: 16 squares

Basic Buns

3 ounces margarine or butter
3 ounces honey
2 eggs
2 ounces raisins
8 ounces flour, self-rising
½ cup milk

Cream margarine and honey thoroughly. Add eggs and beat well. Stir in raisins and flour with milk to make dough a dropping consistency. Grease and flour muffin tin. Pour in batter and fill one-half. Bake at 375 degrees for 15 - 20 minutes. Yield: 12

Kissing don't last: cookery do!
George Meredith
1828-1909

Fried Corn Bread

½ cup flour, all-purpose
1 cup yellow corn meal
3 tablespoons sugar
1 teaspoon salt
3 teaspoons baking powder
1 egg, beaten
1 cup milk
2 tablespoons melted shortening, warm
vegetable oil for frying

Combine dry ingredients. Add milk and stir just enough to blend. Add egg and pour in warm shortening. Stir only to blend. Have skillet hot with ⅛ inch vegetable oil. Drop the batter by tablespoonfuls. Brown on each side turning only once. Serve hot! Serves 6 to 8

"A childhood favorite. Especially good eaten with a spoon from a glass of cold sweetmilk."

Say Again HUSH PUPPIES

1 cup flour, self-rising
1½ cups yellow corn meal
2 tablespoons sugar
½ teaspoon salt
1 egg
1 cup buttermilk
1 small onion, finely grated
Oil for deep fryer

Combine flour, corn meal, salt and sugar. Add egg, buttermilk and onion and mix well. Form into balls the size of small eggs and drop into hot oil in deep fryer. Brown evenly about 3 - 5 minutes. Drain on paper towels and serve hot. Serves: 6

*"Fly the Airplane First
Talk second"*

JIM BELL

Reported Delicious Oatmeal Pancakes

1¾ cups buttermilk
1½ cups quick rolled oats
1 teaspoon soda
½ cup flour, all-purpose
2 teaspoons sugar
1 teaspoon salt
3 eggs, beaten
¼ cup raisins, optional
¼ cup Airborne Granola*, optional

Combine buttermilk and oats in mixing bowl. Combine and sift dry ingredients and add to oats. Add the beaten eggs and beat well. Fold in optional raisins if you prefer or granola. (Granola will give the batter a nutty-raisin flavor and improve texture.) Serves: 4

*(See index)

SWEET
BREADS

Sweet Bread: Amelia

1 8-ounce package chopped dates
1 cup hot water
1 cup sugar
1 stick butter
1 teaspoon soda
2 eggs
1 teaspoon vanilla extract
1¾ cup flour, all-purpose
2 teaspoons cocoa
½ teaspoon salt
1 6-ounce package chocolate chips (semi-sweet)
1 cup pecans, chopped finely

Cover dates with hot water. Let stand. Cream sugar, butter and soda; add eggs and vanilla and mix well. Sift flour, cocoa and salt; add alternately with the date mixture. Turn dough into 9 x 13 inch baking pan lightly greased. Sprinkle chocolate chips and pecans over top. Bake at 350 degrees for 35 minutes. Yield: 12 servings

"Take one bite and you will be sure to return!"

*More are men's ends
mark'd than their lives
before. The setting sun,
and the music at the
close, As the last taste
Of sweets, is sweetest
last, Writ in remembrance
more than things long
past.*

GAUNT
William Shakespeare

Orange Muffins

1½ sticks butter, softened
1⅔ cups sugar
3 eggs, beaten
½ cup orange juice
grated rind of 2 oranges
1 teaspoon vanilla extract
2½ cups flour, all-purpose (sifted)
2 teaspoons baking powder
½ teaspoon salt
powdered sugar

Cream butter, sugar and eggs well. Add juice, rind and vanilla. Mix well. Add sifted dry ingredients. Stir lightly until batter is only slightly moist, but lumpy. Pour into greased and floured muffin tins or paper muffin cups placed in muffin tin. Fill ½ full and bake at 350 degrees for 15 - 20 minutes. Remove and dust with powdered sugar. Yield: 2 dozen

Blueberry Muffins

1 cup sugar, superfine
½ stick butter
1 cup milk
1 egg
1⅓ cups flour, all purpose
¼ teaspoon salt
2 teaspoons baking powder
¾ teaspoon cinnamon
¾ teaspoon nutmeg
½ teaspoon vanilla extract
1 cup fresh or frozen blueberries, thawed and
    drained

Cream sugar and butter on low speed until smooth. Add milk, egg, and ⅔ cup flour, baking powder, cinnamon, nutmeg, vanilla and salt. Mix well, but not overly blended. Gently mix in remaining ⅔ cup flour. Batter should be lumpy. Gently fold in blueberries. Use paper liners in muffin tins and fill ¾ full. Bake at 375 degrees for 20 - 30 minutes. Makes 12 muffins.
(To make superfine sugar, place sugar in food processor and swirl for a few seconds.)

Cinnamon Muffins

1½ cups flour, all-purpose
pinch of salt
2 teaspoons baking powder
1 tablespoon cinnamon
½ cup butter,melted
1 cup sugar
2 eggs
½ cup milk

Sift flour with baking powder, salt and cinnamon. Cream butter, sugar and eggs thoroughly. Stir in the flour mixture alternately with the milk. Pour into greased muffin tins and bake at 350 degrees for 25 minutes. Yield: 18 muffins. Cool. Frost with Cinnamon Frosting below.

Cinnamon Frosting:
Mix 1 cup whipping cream with ¼ cup sugar. Chill for 2 hours in refrigerator. Beat until stiff and add ½ teaspoon cinnamon.

Ginger Bread to Go

1½ cups flour, all-purpose
1½ teaspoons baking soda
¼ teaspoon salt
½ teaspoon cinnamon
½ teaspoon ginger
¼ teaspoon cloves
1 egg
1 cup light molasses
1 stick butter, melted
½ cup hot water

Sift flour with baking soda, salt and spices. Beat egg with molasses, butter and ½ cup hot water until well mixed. Gradually add flour mixture. Beat until smooth. Pour into 8 inch square pan greased lightly and dusted with flour. Bake at 375 degrees for 25 minutes. Cool in pan. Top with Lemon Sauce or dust with powdered sugar. Serves 6 - 8

"This is good old-fashioned Ginger Bread"

Lemon Sauce:
⅔ cup sugar
2 tablespoons flour
1 cup boiling water
2 tablespoons butter
2½ tablespoons lemon juice (about 1 lemon)

Combine sugar and flour in sauce pan. Add water. Cook on medium-low heat until thick. Stir to blend. Add butter and lemon juice. Stir until smooth. Grated lemon rind may be added for more lemon flavor. Yield: Sufficient to cover Ginger Bread.

I saw him even now going
the way of all flesh, that is
to say towards the kitchen.

BIRDLIME
John Webster

Mango Bread

½ cup sugar
½ cup brown sugar
½ cup butter
2 eggs
1 teaspoon lemon extract
1 teaspoon vanilla extract
2 cups flour, all-purpose
½ cup wheat germ
1 teaspoon baking powder
½ teaspoon salt
1 teaspoon baking soda
1 ½ teaspoon cinnamon
1 cup mango pulp
½ cup evaporated milk
1 cup raisins
1 cup pecans, chopped

Cream sugars and butter together until light and fluffy. Add eggs one at a time; beating after each. Add lemon and vanilla extract. Sift dry ingredients and add alternately with mango pulp and milk. Add raisins and nuts. Pour into greased loaf pan. Bake at 350 degrees for 1 hour. Yield: 1 loaf

Mango Muffins

4 tablespoons butter
⅓ cup sugar
1 egg
1 cup milk
1 cup mango pulp
2 cups flour, all-purpose
¼ teaspoon salt
4 teaspoons baking powder
¼ teaspoon nutmeg

Cream butter, sugar and egg until light and fluffy. Add milk and mango pulp and beat well. Sift dry ingredients and stir into batter only enough to moisten. Pour into greased muffin pan and bake at 400 degrees for 25 - 30 minutes. Yield: 12 muffins.

"We love you, Mango"

Oatmeal Muffins

1 cup quick cooking oats
1 cup buttermilk
1 egg
½ cup brown sugar
1 cup flour, all-purpose
1 teaspoon baking powder
1 teaspoon salt
½ teaspoon soda
⅓ cup butter, melted and cooled

Combine oats with buttermilk. Beat in egg. Stir in brown sugar. Sift flour, baking powder, salt and soda. Add to oat mixture. Pour into greased muffin tin. Bake at 400 degrees for 20 minutes. Yield: 12 muffins

Bran Muffins

1½ cups Bran Flake Cereal
1¼ cups milk
1 egg
⅓ cup vegetable oil
1 cup flour, all-purpose
¼ cup unprocessed bran
3 teaspoons baking powder
½ teaspoon salt
½ cup sugar
5 dashes nutmeg
¼ cup raisins, optional

In small bowl combine bran flakes with milk to soak. In small bowl beat the egg with the vegetable oil. In mixing bowl combine flour, bran, baking powder, salt, sugar and nutmeg. Stir to blend dry ingredients. Add the bran flake mixture and the egg mixture. Add raisins if desired and stir only to blend. Pour into greased muffin tin and bake at 400 degrees for 25 minutes. Yield: 12 large or 36 small muffins. Skim milk may be substituted.

"These muffins are so good. You never get bored with them. I made them every week for two years."

Bravo Banana Bread

1 stick butter or margarine
1 cup sugar
2 eggs
1 cup banana, mashed
1½ tablespoon milk
1 teaspoon fresh lemon juice
1 teaspoon banana liqueur
2 cups flour, all-purpose
1½ teaspoons baking powder
¼ teaspoon salt
½ teaspoon soda
1 cup pecans, chopped

Cream butter, sugar and eggs using a mixer. In separate dish mash banana and add milk and lemon juice. Stir to mix. Add to butter sugar mixture and beat well. Add banana liqueur and mix well. Sift dry ingredients and add to batter; stirring only enough to blend. Fold in nuts. Bake in greased loaf pan at 350 degrees for 1 hour or three small loaf pans at 350 degrees for 35 minutes. Yield: 1 regular size loaf or 3 small loaves. Freezes well.

Note: Over ripe bananas have more flavor. They are easily frozen, peeling and all in a freezer bag. Easily defrosted by placing in microwave oven for 2 minutes.

*"I mix them with my
brains, sir."*

SAMUEL SMILES, SELF HELP
John Opie, 1761-1807

Pumpkin Bread

3 cups sugar
1 cup cooking oil
3 eggs
1 16-ounce can pumpkin or 2 cups fresh
3 cups flour, all-purpose
½ teaspoon salt
½ teaspoon baking powder
1 teaspoon baking soda
1 teaspoon cloves
1 teaspoon cinnamon
1 teaspoon nutmeg
1 cup pecans, chopped

Cream sugar, oil and eggs. Add pumpkin and sifted dry ingredients. Fold in nuts. Pour into greased tube pan or two greased loaf pans. Bake at 350 degrees for 1 hour and 15 minutes. Yield: 2 loaves

On the coast of Coromandel
where the early pumpkins blow,
In the middle of the woods
Lived the Yonghy-Bonghy-Bo.

THE COURTSHIP OF THE YONGHY-BONGHY-BO'
Edward Lear, 1812-1888

Tea Cakes

4 tablespoons butter
2 eggs, beaten
1 cup sugar
2 cups flour, all-purpose
2 teaspoons baking powder
½ teaspoon vanilla extract

Cream butter and eggs; add sugar and mix well. Add flour, baking powder and extract; mix well. Form into a ball and roll out on floured dough board. Cut with tea cake cutters. Sprinkle with sugar if desired. Bake at 450 degrees 10 - 12 minutes.
Yield: 1 dozen

"I do like a little bit of butter to
     my bread."

WHEN WE WERE VERY YOUNG
A. A. Milne

– Notes –

BIG DIPPER
SOUPS

*"For you there's rosemary
and rue; these keep seeming
and savour all the winter
long."*

THE WINTER'S TALE
Shakespeare

Chicken Stock A la Wing Tips

5½ pounds chicken, wing tips, necks and backs
3 onions, each studded with a clove
1 large carrot, chopped
2 ribs celery, chopped
4 black peppercorns
1 bay leaf
½ teaspoon salt
½ teaspoon thyme

Combine all ingredients in 6 quart stock pot with enough water to cover. Bring to a boil over high heat, skimming off foam as it rises to surface. Reduce heat, cover partially and simmer 4 - 5 hours. Strain and return liquid to pot. Boil over high heat until stock is reduced and flavor intensified. Taste and adjust seasoning if necessary. Refrigerate until ready to use. Stock will keep well in refrigerator up to 5 days or 4 months in freezer.

Come, fill the cup, and
*   in the fire of spring*
Your winter garments of repentance
*   fling;*
*   The bird of time has but a*
*   little way to flutter – and*
the bird is on the wing.

Omar Khayyam

Avocado Soup

2 cups peeled, cored and chunked avocado
1 can Chalet Suzanne Chicken Consomme
Condensed reconsitituted with 1 can of water
2 tablespoons lemon juice
1 tablespoon chopped onion
dash pepper
dash hot sauce
½ cup light or heavy cream
salt, if needed

Put all ingredients but cream in blender. Cover and blend until avocado liquifies. Add cream and continue to blend until well mixed. Chill well before serving. Garnish with freshly ground pepper, chopped chives, parsley or thinly sliced lemon. Makes 8 servings.

This has a wonderful, velvety-smooth consistency, especially when heavy cream is used.

Chalet Suzanne
RESTAURANT & COUNTRY INN

U. S. 27 North
LAKE WALES,
FLORIDA

Cream of Garlic Soup

3 ounces salted butter
¾ pound cubed Vermont ham
7 cloves garlic, peeled
2 leeks - the white part cleaned and chopped
1 large potato, peeled and quartered
1½ quarts poultry or rabbit stock
1½ pints heavy cream
salt and white pepper
chopped parsley

Melt butter in sauce pan. Add ham, garlic, chopped leek, potato and simmer for 5 - 10 minutes. Add stock. Cover and simmer for two hours. Puree in food processor. Add heavy cream and salt and pepper to taste. Re-heat before serving. Garnish with parsley. Serves: 6 - 8

Hemingway's
RESTAURANT

PO BOX 337 ROUTE 4 KILLINGTON VT 05751 phone: (802)422-3886

NEEDLE SPLIT Pea Soup

1 package dried split peas
2 quarts water, cold
1 onion, chopped
2 ribs celery, sliced
1 carrot, sliced
1 ham bone
1 bay leaf
3 cups milk
2 tablespoons butter
1½ teaspoons salt
⅛ teaspoon white pepper
dash of nutmeg

Wash and soak peas in cold water overnight. Place peas in a stockpot and add onion, celery, carrot, ham bone, bay leaf and water to cover. Bring to a boil and simmer partially covered until peas are tender (about 2 hours). Remove bone and bay leaf. Puree the soup in a blender or food processor. Return to stockpot and add milk, butter and seasonings. Heat on low heat (do not boil). Serve hot. Serves: 8

Dip into Yogurt Mushroom Soup

1 pound fresh mushrooms, sliced finely
3 cups chicken broth
1 tablespoon fresh parsley, chopped
1 cup plain yogurt

Cook mushrooms in chicken broth for 5 minutes. Remove from heat. Add parsley and yogurt. Serve hot. Serves: 4

Go For It Corn Chowder

¼ cup onion, chopped
1 tablespoon butter
2 tablespoons flour, all-purpose
4 cups milk or half and half
1 teaspoon salt
½ teaspoon white pepper
dash paprika
1 12-ounce can creamed corn

Saute onion in butter until clear and tender. Stir in flour to blend and gradually add the milk. Add remaining ingredients. Heat thoroughly, but do not boil. Serves: 6
Note: Skim milk may be substituted.

The Art of Choking Soup

2 large artichokes, bottoms only
8 cups chicken stock
½ cup hazelnuts
½ cup flour, all-purpose
1 cup half and half
1½ tablespoons sherry
salt and pepper to taste

Steam artichoke bottoms for 1 hour. Combine with 6 cups chicken stock in large saucepan. Toast hazelnuts for 10 minutes at 300 degrees. Cool and remove brown skins. Return nuts to oven and toast about 10 minutes until golden. Remove from oven and crush fine in food processor. Add to artichoke bottoms and simmer for 35 minutes. Puree in food processor or blender and return to saucepan. Combine flour with the two remaining cups of chicken stock blending well until smooth. Add to soup. Add high heat and stir to a boil. Reduce heat and simmer for 15 - 20 minutes. Add cream and salt and pepper. Blend in sherry before serving. Serves: 6

Continental Cauliflower Soup

1 fresh cauliflower, trimmed and destalked
1 chicken bouillon cube
½ cup water
2 cups milk
¼ teaspoon dried basil
dash white pepper
1 tablespoon dried parsley
¼ cup Swiss cheese, shredded

Cook cauliflower on low heat with dissolved bouillon cube and water; covered. (about 5 minutes). Place in blender with all other ingredients except the cheese. Blend until smooth. Reheat gently and add cheese. Serve hot as soup or sauce. Serves: 4

Gullet GLIDE Gazpacho

2 cucumbers
4 medium tomatoes, ripe
2 large onions
2 green peppers
1 cup wine vinegar
1 cup olive oil
1 cup water
1 clove garlic, minced
1 teaspoon salt
1 tablespoon Tabasco
2 tablespoons chives, chopped
1 tablespoon mayonnaise
1 12-ounce bottle ketchup

Set aside ½ cucumber, 1½ tomatoes, ½ onion and ½ green pepper. Dice in ¼ inch cubes. Place in individual hors d'oeuvre dishes and refrigerate until ready to serve as garnish choices to top soup.

Soup: Chop remaining cucumbers, tomatoes, onions and green peppers. Place in a glass container with vinegar, oil, water, garlic, salt, Tabasco and chives. Let stand 2 hours. Puree in blender or food processor, adding a little more water if necessary. Strain and add mayonnaise and ketchup. Blend thoroughly. Serve with chilled garnishes.

Note: High in vitamins and low in calories. The flavor improves with keeping with no loss of food value. "An excellent choice for a flying picnic."

Squash Bisque Bi-Plane

1 cup onion, chopped
¼ cup carrot, grated
4 tablespoons butter
2 potatoes, diced and cooked
1 pound fresh summer squash, cut in chunks
2 cups chicken broth
1 carton half and half
½ cup whipping cream
1 teaspoon salt
⅛ teaspoon red pepper

Saute onion and carrot with butter in heavy pot. Cook slowly, covered until soft. Cook potatoes until just tender in separate pot. Add cooked potatoes, squash and broth to onion mixture. Cover and simmer until tender. Puree in blender or food processor. Return to heavy pot and add half and half, cream, salt and pepper. Slowly heat thoroughly. Do not boil. Serves: 8

Note: To change texture, reserve part of the boiled potatoes and stir in as served. "J. B. and Julie love to find potato 'lumps' in their soup."

★

☆

Taxi to RAMP Soup

½ bushel ramps
4 large onions, sliced thinly
1½ cups butter
1 cup flour, all-purpose
12 10½-ounce cans beef broth
3 lemons
2 ounces worcestershire sauce
12 ounces dry vermouth
10 soup cans water
salt and pepper to taste
6 ounces Scotch

Ramp or wild leek is a native wild onion that some people prefer instead of the leeks available in the market. The flat leaves grow from the ground in spring and by summer produce a leafless flowering stem bearing greenish-white flowers. It is during this time that Ramps may be dug with a pick in order to reach the important bulb. Remove the bulb, clean and slice thinly. Discard the green tops and leaves. Clairfy the ramps and onion slices in ½ cup butter. Make a roux: Stir flour into ⅔ cup butter in a heavy skillet until brown-beige (do not burn). Gradually add beef broth until the roux can be poured into a large stockpot. Add remainder of broth, ramps and onion mixture, juice of the lemons, worcestershire sauce and vermouth. Stir well. Add water. Sample for taste and add salt and pepper to taste. Simmer 6 hours partially covered. Cool and refrigerate. Remove surface butter. Freeze at this point if desired. To serve: heat scotch in a saucepan and ignite. Immediately pour into soup, stirring rapidly to burn off alcohol. Allow soup to simmer uncovered 30 minutes.
Yield: 1½ Gallons

Thermos Vichyssoise

4 tablespoons butter
3 leeks, white part sliced
1 onion, chopped
2 ribs celery, chopped
1 teaspoon parsley
2 cups chicken broth
2 potatoes, peeled and diced
1 teaspoon salt
1 carton half and half cream
1 tablespoon chopped chives
⅛ teaspoon white pepper

In a large soup pot melt the butter, add the leeks, onion and celery. Cook on low heat about 15 minutes until tender, but not brown. Add the parsley, stock, potatoes and salt. Partially cover and cook until potatoes are tender (about 15 minutes). Puree in blender or food processor and return to soup pot. Stir in half and half, chives and white pepper. Serve hot or cold. Serves: 4 - 6

Supersonic Spinach Soup

1 onion, chopped
2 cloves garlic, minced
1 tablespoon vegetable oil
3 cups water
1 large potato, diced
1 teaspoon salt
½ teaspoon white pepper
¼ teaspoon nutmeg
1 cup chicken broth
2 cups fresh spinach, rinsed and dried
1 cup heavy cream
2 tablespoons lemon juice

In a large soup pot cook the onion and garlic in the oil over low heat until tender. Add water, potato, salt, pepper, nutmeg and broth. Bring to a boil and simmer covered until the potato is tender. Add the spinach and cook 2 - 3 minutes. Puree in blender. Gently blend in cream and lemon juice. Serve hot or cold. Watercress may be substituted for spinach. Serves: 6

"Soup of the evening,
beautiful soup!"

ALICE'S ADVENTURES IN WONDERLAND
Lewis Carroll

– *Notes* –

SALADS
SALAD
DRESSINGS
SAUCES

My salad days,
When I was green in
judgment.

CLEOPATRA
William Shakespeare

CHOPPER Slaw

1 head cabbage, CHOPPED
1 bunch celery, CHOPPED
1 bell pepper, CHOPPED
1 large onion, CHOPPED
½ bag carrots, CHOPPED
2 cans tomatoes, drained and CHOPPED
1 pint vinegar
1 pound light brown sugar
1 tablespoon mustard seed
2 teaspoons salt

Combine the first six ingredients in a large bowl. Boil the vinegar, sugar, mustard seed and salt. Pour the liquid over the slaw mixture and refrigerate overnight. Drain and serve on a lettuce leaf as a salad. Yield: ½ gallon and will easily serve 20.

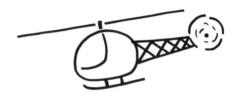

Cruise Cauliflower Cold Slaw

2 cups raw cauliflower, shredded
½ cup onion, chopped
¼ cup green pepper, chopped
2 tablespoons fresh parsley
1½ cups celery, chopped
mayonnaise and sour cream
salt and pepper to taste

Combine and mix all ingredients well. Add half and half mayonnaise and sour cream to moisten. Salt and pepper to taste. Serves: 6

A Sea of Macaroni Salad

1 pound macaroni or shells
1 cup celery, chopped
1 cup green pepper, chopped
½ cup onion, chopped
2 tablespoons cider vinegar
½ teaspoon sugar
½ teaspoon salt
dash black pepper
3 cans medium shrimp, cut in half
    Reserve liquid from 2 cans
2 6½-ounce cans tuna, drained
1 quart mayonnaise

Prepare macaroni according to package directions; drain. Combine remaining ingredients with warm macaroni; stir to blend. Serves: 15
"Wonderfully delicious."

A special family recipe from my friend and flight student, Beverly Stayton Wolf.

Phonetic Alphabet Salad

2 cups canned orange and grapefruit sections
1 7-ounce bottle ginger ale
1 tablespoon lemon juice
1 3-ounce package orange gelatin
1 3-ounce package lemon gelatin
¼ teaspoon salt
2 cups water, boiling hot
1 8-ounce package alphabet macaroni
1 tablespoon orange rind, grated
1 cup creamed cottage cheese
1 cup prunes, cooked and chopped

Continued on next page →

Phonetic Alphabet Salad (Continued)

Drain fruit sections and set aside (reserve syrup). Combine syrup with ginger ale to make 1¾ cups liquid. Add lemon juice; set aside. Dissolve gelatins and salt in boiling water. Stir gelatin mixture into syrup mixture; blend. Cook macaroni according to package directions; drain and rinse with cold water. Add rind and cottage cheese to gelatin-syrup mixture. Stir in fruit sections, macaroni and prunes. Pour into lightly greased 9 inch square pan. Chill until firm. Serves: 8

"Affirmative, you will get a BRAVO"

Wilted Exhaust Salad

6 slices bacon
1 head Boston or leaf lettuce, washed and dried
1 medium onion, sliced thinly
¼ cup cider vinegar
1½ teaspoons sugar
½ teaspoon dry mustard
¼ teaspoon salt
2 dashes black pepper
2 eggs, hard boiled and sliced for garnish

Fry bacon until crisp in a large skillet. Remove bacon and drain on paper towels; crumble. Remove and discard all but ¼ cup bacon drippings. Tear lettuce into bite-size pieces and combine with onion and bacon in a large salad bowl. Add vinegar, sugar, mustard, salt and pepper to bacon drippings. Heat to boiling and stir to loosen browned bits. Remove from heat and add lettuce mixture. Toss until lettuce is slightly wilted, exhausted and coated with dressing. Return to salad bowl and garnish with egg slices. Serves: 6

Untighten Your Seat Belt
Macaroni Salad

1 16-ounce package elbow macaroni
2 eggs, boiled and chopped
¼ cup green pepper, chopped
¼ cup onion, chopped (optional)
1 2-ounce jar pimentos, chopped and drained
¼ cup celery, chopped
½ cup sweet pickle relish
mayonnaise to blend
salt and black pepper to taste

Prepare macaroni according to package directions; drain. Combine with remaining ingredients; stir to blend. Serve warm or cold. Keep chilled. Serves: 6 - 8

Spirit of St. Louis Salad Dressing

2 garlic cloves, minced
1 onion, chopped
1 cup mayonnaise
¼ cup chili sauce
¼ cup tomato catsup
1 teaspoon worcestershire sauce
1 teaspoon black pepper
¼ cup olive oil
2 tablespoons water, cold
1 teaspoon prepared yellow mustard
dash Tabasco
dash paprika

Combine all ingredients in a food processor or blender and blend well. Keep well chilled in a covered container. Yields: 1 pint

Windsock Salad

2 cups NORTHERN green beans, drained
2 cups SOUTHERN English peas, drained
4 large EASTERN celery ribs, chopped
1 can WESTERN water chestnuts, sliced and
    drained
1 4-ounce can pimientos, chopped
½ cup green onions, chopped

Dressing:

2 cups olive oil
½ cup sugar
½ cup apple cider vinegar
2 tablespoons worcestershire sauce
1 teaspoon salt
½ teaspoon garlic salt
½ teaspoon dry mustard
juice of 2 lemons
juice of 1 orange

Mix oil, sugar and vinegar until blended. Add remaining
ingredients and mix well. Pour over vegetables and marinate
overnight covered in refrigerator. Drain and serve as vegetables if
winds are light and variable, otherwise, serve as a salad on
GUSTY greens. Serve chilled. Yield: 6 servings

WIND SOCK
SALAD

Crafty Cranberry Salad

1 large can whole berry cranberry sauce
1 3-ounce package cream cheese, cubed
1 small can crushed pineapple
water
1 tablespoon plain gelatin
1 6-ounce package raspberry gelatin
2 cups water, boiling
7 ice cubes
½ cup pecans, chopped finely

In a small sauce pan combine sauce with cream cheese on medium low heat; stir to blend. Drain pineapple and reserve liquid. Add pineapple to cream cheese mixture and remove from heat; set aside. Combine pineapple liquid with water to make 1 cup; add plain gelatin and stir to dissolve; set aside. Mix raspberry gelatin with boiling water; stir to dissolve. Add ice cubes; mix well until blended. Combine all 3 mixtures in a 4 quart lightly greased mold. Refrigerate until thickened (2 - 3 hours). Fold in nuts. Refrigerate overnight to set. Serve chilled.
Serves: 8

An Elegant Mixture

1 large can pears
1 3-ounce package lime gelatin
3 tablespoons mayonnaise
1 6-ounce package cream cheese
½ pint whipping cream, whipped

Drain pears; reserve 1 cup liquid. Heat liquid and dissolve gelatin. Refrigerate to chill slightly. Combine mayonnaise, cream cheese and pears in a blender. Blend until smooth. Combine pear mixture with chilled gelatin and fold in whipped cream. Pour into 2 quart mold lightly greased. Chill until set.
Serves: 6

Chicken Salad To Fly

3 whole chicken breasts
3 ribs celery, chopped
4 peppercorns
½ teaspoon salt
2 eggs, boiled and chopped finely
¼ cup sweet pickle relish
mayonnaise
salt and pepper to taste
sliced almonds, optional

Boil chicken breasts in enough water to cover with 1 rib of celery, peppercorns and salt until tender. Allow chicken to cool in cooking juices. Remove skin and bone. Chop chicken into chunks or grind coarsely. Combine with remaining ingredients including the remaining 2 ribs of celery; mix well. Keep well chilled. Serves: 4

Sky Peek Potato Salad

4 large baking potatoes, boiled, peeled and diced
3 eggs, boiled and chopped
½ cup sweet pickle relish
1 2-ounce jar pimentos, chopped and drained
⅓ cup green pepper, chopped
1 small carrot, shredded
⅓ cup purple onion, optional
¼ cup prepared yellow mustard
1 cup mayonnaise
salt and pepper to taste

Combine first 7 ingredients in a large mixing bowl. In a small bowl blend mustard and mayonnaise. Pour over potato mixture and stir to blend. Taste for seasoning. Keep well chilled. Serves: 6

Home-made Mayonnaise

2 egg yolks, room temperature
2 tablespoons lemon juice
2 cups vegetable oil
1½ teaspoons prepared mustard
½ teaspoon white pepper
1 teaspoon salt
⅛ teaspoon red pepper
⅛ teaspoon paprika
16 drops Tabasco, optional

Using an electric mixer with small bowl, beat egg yolks until thick. Slowly add a few drops of lemon juice and then a few drops of oil. Keep the mixer on high and keep adding the oil and lemon juice slowly and alternately. As the mixture thickens add more generously. Beat in the mustard. Reduce to medium speed and add seasonings. Yield: 2½ cups. Keep chilled.
"Delicious with hot fried shrimp."
Special tip: Once the egg mixture starts to thicken, discontinue adding the lemon juice and continue small steady flow of oil until adding all of the oil. Then, add the remaining lemon juice, etc.

BONANZA Salad

2 cups mixed greens
3 radishes, sliced
4 green onions, chopped
½ cup cabbage, shredded
½ cup cauliflower, sliced
¼ cup green pepper, sliced
¼ cup red pepper, sliced
¼ cup summer squash, sliced
¼ cup broccoli, chopped

Toss and mix with favorite salad dressing. "We prefer vinaigrette."

Clear and Unrestricted
Remoulade Sauce

12 ounces mayonnaise
3 ounces creole brown mustard
1 ounce prepared yellow mustard
½ cup green pepper, chopped
¼ cup green onions with tops, chopped
½ cup celery, chopped
¼ cup fresh parsley, chopped
4 garlic cloves, minced
1 ounce anchovy filets, chopped
juice of 2 lemons
1 ounce horseradish
dash accent
¼ teaspoon salt
2 tablespoons worcestershire sauce

Place ingredients in a blender and blend until smooth (about 1 minute). Pour into a covered container and chill 3 hours before serving. Yield: 1 pint

Fully ASPIRATED Aspic

1 3-ounce package lemon gelatin
1¼ cups water, hot
1 8-ounce can tomato sauce
1½ tablespoons cider vinegar
1 teaspoon salt
black pepper to taste
⅓ cup cucumber, peeled and chopped

Dissolve gelatin in water. Stir in tomato sauce. Blend in vinegar, salt and pepper. Pour into 2 quart mold. Chill until partially set (about 2 hours). Fold in cucumbers; chill until set.
Serves: 4

Foggy Fruit Salad Dressing

1 14-ounce carton Ricotta cheese
2 fresh mangos, peeled and seeded
¼ cup fresh lemon juice
4 tablespoons raw honey
1 teaspoon poppy seed, optional

Combine and blend all ingredients in a food processor or blender. Chill to thicken and serve with fresh fruit. Yield: 1 pint

"The fog comes
on little cat feet.
It sits looking
over the harbor and city
on silent haunches
and then moves on."
Carl Sandburg

Orville Orange Sherbet Salad

1 3-ounce package orange gelatin
¾ cup water, boiling
1 pint orange sherbet
1 cup sour cream
1 3-ounce package lemon gelatin
1 cup water, boiling
1 11-ounce can mandarin orange segments

Dissolve orange gelatin in ¾ cup water. Add sherbet; stir until blended. Pour mixture into a 4 quart lightly greased mold and chill for 1 hour. Spread sour cream layer on top. Dissolve lemon gelatin in water; set aside. Drain orange segments and reserve liquid. Add enough water to make 1 cup; set aside. Combine orange segments, lemon gelatin and orange segment liquid. Chill until almost set (2 hours). Place on top of sour cream layer in mold. Chill for 8 - 10 hours. Serves: 8

TCA Layered Salad

6 cups mixed greens, torn into bite-size pieces
1 10-ounce package frozen green peas
¼ cup green onion, chopped
1 small can water chestnuts, drained and sliced
salt and pepper to taste
2 cups mayonnaise
2 cups Swiss cheese, shredded
½ pound bacon, cooked, drained and crumbled
6 eggs, boiled and sliced
¼ cup green onion tops, chopped
¼ teaspoon paprika

In a large deep glass salad bowl begin layers starting with greens. Add peas, onion, water chestnuts and salt and pepper. Spread a layer of mayonnaise, sprinkle cheese and bacon; place eggs. Garnish top with green onion tops and sprinkle paprika. Cover and chill 3 hours before serving. Serves: 8 - 10

"A favorite at the 'Aunt Hill' reunion from Aunt Martha."

CREW Cut Cabbage Slaw

1 cabbage, shredded finely
1 large white onion, sliced finely and rings
    separated
½ green pepper, grated
salt and pepper to taste
½ cup sugar
1 cup mayonnaise
¼ cup white vinegar

In a large bowl combine cabbage, onion and green pepper; toss gently. Add salt and pepper. Sprinkle sugar. Combine mayonnaise and vinegar; mix well. Pour over cabbage mixture. Toss well and chill. Serves: 8 - 10

Salad A La PREFERRED ROOT

1 cup sugar
½ cup water
½ cup vinegar
6 cloves
2 tablespoons gelatin, unflavored
½ cup beet juice
1 No. 2 can chopped beets, drain and reserve
   liquid
1 can mandarine slices, drained
1 cup walnuts, chopped
sour cream, mayonnaise, yogurt

Combine sugar, water, vinegar and cloves in a small saucepan and boil for 10 minutes. Remove the cloves. Soften gelatin in beet juice; let stand 5 minutes. Combine boiled mixture with gelatin. Cool. Add beets, mandarine slices and nuts. Pour into mold and chill until set (3 - 4 hours). Serve with sour cream, mayonnaise or yogurt or combination. Serve chilled.
Serves: 4 - 6

Hot Sweet Mustard

1 8-ounce Colman's dry mustard
12 ounces tarragon vinegar
3 eggs, beaten
1 cup sugar

Place mustard and vinegar in top of double boiler; soak until blended. Beat eggs and sugar in blender and add to mustard mixture. Cook in double boiler until thick. Pour into covered container and keep refrigerated. Yield: 1 pint

"This makes everything good, especially turkey, beef or ham."

Captain's Choice Chef Salad

2 cups mixed greens, washed and drained
½ cup celery, chopped
1 small red pepper, cut in strips
1 avocado, sliced
3 ounces cheddar cheese, grated
2 eggs, boiled and quartered
½ pound shrimp, boiled and peeled
3 ounces turkey, cooked and sliced in strips
3 ounces ham, cooked and sliced in strips

Assemble and toss ingredients onto greens. Serve chilled with choice of dressing. " We like Clear and Unrestricted Remoulade Sauce." Serves: 4

Sunset Remoulade Sauce

½ cup onions, chopped
¾ cup vegetable oil
¼ cup tarragon vinegar
½ cup brown creole mustard
2 teaspoons paprika
¾ teaspoon red pepper
2 teaspoons salt
2 garlic cloves, minced
½ cup green onions with tops, chopped

Place ingredients in a blender and blend for 15 seconds; stop and scrape down sides with a rubber spatula each 5 seconds. Pour into container, cover and keep chilled. Yield: 1 pint

"Excellent with chilled seafood."

Circuit Breaker Onions

2 large Bermuda onions, sliced thinly
water, boiling hot
water, ice cold
4 tablespoons olive oil
4 tablespoons red wine vinegar
4 tablespoons hot pepper sauce

Place onions in a mixing bowl and cover with boiling water; drain. Immediately place into a second bowl of ice cold water. Let stand until cooled. Combine remaining ingredients in a small bowl; whisk to blend. Drain onion and place on paper towels to remove excess water. Separate slices into rings. Pour marinade over rings; stir. Refrigerate covered for 8 hours; stir well after first 3 hours. Serve chilled or at room temperature. Serves: 4

Vinaigrette Dressing

4 tablespoons red wine vinegar
½ teaspoon salt
1 tablespoon Dijon-style mustard
½ cup olive oil
3 garlic cloves, minced
1 tablespoon fresh lemon juice
minced parsley to taste

Whisk vinegar and salt into mustard. Slowly whisk in olive oil. Add garlic and lemon juice. Blend and add parsley. Whisk again before serving. Serves: 4

PLANE PASTA

PAPA Pasta Pronto

1 8-ounce package fettuccini
2 tablespoons butter
1 small onion, chopped
6-ounces Canadian bacon, sliced
½ pound fresh asparagus
1¼ cups heavy cream
½ cup parmesan cheese, grated
black pepper to taste
dash of vegetable seasoning
additional parmesan

Cook fettucine according to package directions; drain. Melt butter in medium size skillet and cook onions until soft (about 3 minutes). Add bacon and brown slightly. Add asparagus, cover, reduce heat and simmer until asparagus is tender (about 5 - 7 minutes). In a small saucepan bring cream to a boil for 2 minutes to reduce slightly. Remove from heat and stir in cheese. Add cream mixture to asparagus mixture; add pepper and vegetable seasoning. Simmer 2 minutes. Pour sauce over fettuccini. Serve hot with additional parmesan. Serves: 6
Note: Frozen asparagus may be substituted.

"A special recipe from a very special person, Diane Sehrt."

*My shoulder was frozen
And ached with pains
She used "spray and stretch"
to release my shoulder reins.*

*So if ever you wonder
And cannot believe
How I can fly 'round
The country 'n glee*

*Remember the therapy
from Diane of Jefferson
Then you will know
Where I get my propulsion.*

Marlene Morris

Shrimp Fettuccini

3 onions, chopped finely
2 green peppers, chopped finely
¼ cup celery, chopped finely
1½ cups butter
¼ cup flour, all-purpose
4 tablespoons dried parsley
2 pounds fresh shrimp, peeled and deveined
1 pint heavy cream
1 pound jalapeno Velveeta cheese, cut into small
    pieces
2 garlic cloves, minced
salt to taste
red and white pepper to taste
2 8-ounce packages fettuccini

In a heavy skillet cook onions, green pepper and celery in butter until tender. Add flour and cook 10 - 15 minutes while stirring to blend. Add parsley and shrimp. Cover and cook 12 - 15 minutes; stir frequently. Add cream, cheese, garlic, salt and pepper. Cover and cook on low heat 30 minutes and stir occasionally. Prepare fettuccini according to package directions; drain. Combine fettuccini and shrimp mixture. Toss well and serve hot.
Serves: 8

Lasagna Roll-Ups

8 lasagna strips
1 tablespoon olive oil
1 medium onion, chopped
2 garlic cloves, minced
1 16-ounce can tomatoes, cut in pieces
1 6-ounce can tomato paste
3 ounces water
1 tablespoon fresh parsley, chopped
1½ teaspoons salt
1½ teaspoons sugar
1 teaspoon oregano leaves
1 teaspoon basil
¼ teaspoon black pepper
1 16-ounce carton ricotta cheese
1 cup mozzarella cheese, grated
⅓ cup parmesan cheese, grated
2 eggs, beaten
1 teaspoon salt
1 cup mozzarella cheese, grated (for top)
½ tablespoon fresh parsley, chopped (for top)

Prepare lasagna strips according to package directions; drain and rinse under cold water. In a large skillet heat oil and cook onion and garlic until tender. Add next 9 ingredients; reduce heat and simmer 20 minutes. In a small bowl blend ricotta, mozzarella, parmesan, eggs, parsley and salt. Spread cheese mixture equally over lasagna strips. Roll up each strip. Pour ½ of the sauce in the bottom of a 2 quart lasagna pan; arrange lasagna rolls seam side down in pan and top with remaining sauce, mozzarella and parsley. Cover and bake at 350 degrees for 40 minutes. Serves: 6

Short-Cut Lasagna

1 pound ground chuck
1 tablespoon vegetable oil
1 16-ounce can tomatoes
1 8-ounce can tomato sauce
1 15½-ounce jar Ragu spaghetti sauce
2 garlic cloves, minced
½ teaspoon oregano
salt to taste
1 8-ounce package lasagna
1 6-ounce package mozzarella cheese, sliced
1 cup cottage cheese, cream style
½ cup parmesan cheese, grated

In a medium sized skillet brown chuck in oil; drain. Add next 6 ingredients; cover and simmer 40 minutes. Prepare lasagna according to package directions; drain and rinse under cold water. Place one-half lasagna in a buttered 10 x 8 x 2 inch baking dish. Cover lasagna with ⅓ of the sauce. Place a layer of cheese slices over the sauce. Spread a layer of cottage cheese. Repeat layers ending with sauce. Sprinkle top with parmesan cheese. Bake at 350 degrees for 30 minutes. Remove and cool slightly. Cut into squares and remove with a spatula to serve. Serves: 6

Parachute Pasta

2½ cups rotini, uncooked
1 tablespoon parsley, minced
½ cup parmesan cheese, grated
vinaigrette dressing

Prepare rotini according to package directions; drain. Toss with parsley, cheese and vinaigrette. Chill or serve at room temperature. Serves: 6

May Day Delight

1 6-ounce package noodles
1 medium cabbage
½ teaspoon salt
½ teaspoon sugar
½ cup water
2 medium onions, chopped
1 stick butter
black pepper to taste

Prepare noodles according to package directions; drain. Cut cabbage into fourths and cook slowly until tender with the salt, sugar and water; drain and chop coarsely. Saute onions with butter until tender and golden. Combine noodles, cabbage and onion mixture. Toss and blend with pepper. Serve hot. Serves: 6

Run-A-Way Rigatoni

1 8-ounce package rigatoni
2 7-ounce cans salmon or tuna
⅔ cup mayonnaise
½ cup pecans, chopped
2 tablespoons lemon juice
¼ teaspoon white pepper
¼ cup green onions, chopped
½ cup fresh parsley, chopped

Prepare rigatoni according to package directions; drain. Combine tuna or salmon with mayonnaise; mix well. Add nuts, lemon juice, pepper and green onions. Mix well. Fill each rigatoni with mixture and dip ends in parsley. Keep chilled until serving time. Yield: 20

PITCH It Pasta

4 medium carrots, peeled and chunky sliced
1 6-ounce package frozen pea pods
1 medium fresh broccoli, stalked and separated
1 16-ounce package Ranch dressing
1 tablespoon basil leaves
1 8-ounce package fettuccini
3 chicken bouillon cubes
½ cup parmesan cheese, grated
fresh parsley

Using a vegetable steamer, cook carrots, pea pods and broccoli together until barely tender; drain. Prepare dressing according to package directions; stir in basil leaves. Prepare fettuccini according to package directions except add bouillon cubes to cooking water; drain. Pitch all three mixtures together and toss gently. Serve hot or room temperature on a large pasta platter. Sprinkle with parmesan cheese and garnish with fresh parsley. Serves: 6 "Delicious"

Shrimp and Jalapeno Pasta

Four #15 - 20 shrimp per person

Cilantro Pesto
> 1 bunch cilantro
> 1 tablespoon minced garlic
> 2 tablespoons white wine
> 1 tablespoon lemon juice
> 1 cup olive oil
> pinch of salt

Place all of the above ingredients (except shrimp) in food processor and blend well.

Jalapeno Pasta
> 3 whole eggs
> 1 egg yolk
> 1 tablespoon olive oil
> 2½ cups flour
> 9 whole, unseeded, jalapeno peppers, finely diced

Pour the flour into the food processor first, then add the rest of the ingredients and mix until you have a firm ball. Refrigerate 1 hour. Then roll the dough out and cut noodles to desired width. Sautee the shrimp in a little olive oil, then add 3 tablespoons of cilantro pesto. Add ½ quart of heavy cream and bring to a boil. Remove from the heat and gently stir in the pasta. Top with 1 cup of grated parmesan cheese. Serves: 6

Chef Arturo Boada
517 Louisiana
Houston, Texas
(713) 224-4438

1985 GRAND AWARD
Wine Spectator Magazine

☆ ☆ ☆ ☆ ☆
5-STAR RESTAURANT
Fisher Annotated Guide

TRAVEL HOLIDAY AWARD
for Dining Disctinction

– *Notes* –

VEGETABLES
and RICE

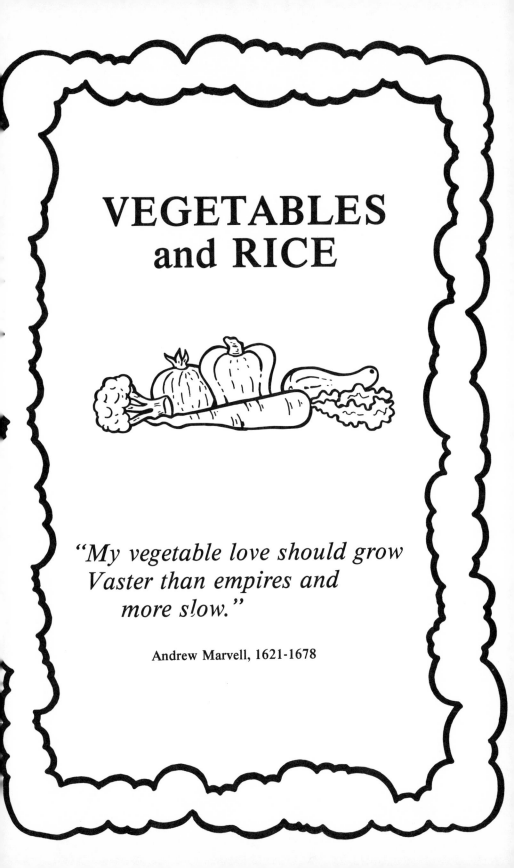

*"My vegetable love should grow
Vaster than empires and
more slow."*

Andrew Marvell, 1621-1678

Identified Glorified Cabbage

1 cabbage head, coarsely cut
1 large onion, chopped finely
¾ stick butter
½ pound Velveeta cheese
1 10¾-ounce can cream of mushroom soup
salt and red pepper to taste
bread crumbs, plain

Boil cabbage in salted water until just tender. Wilt onion in butter and add cheese in hunks. On low heat melt and blend well. Add drained cabbage and cream of mushroom soup. Season to taste with salt and red pepper. Pour into baking dish and cover with bread crumbs. Bake uncovered at 350 degrees for 30 minutes. Serves: 6

'The time has come, 'the Walrus said,
'To talk of many things:
Of shoes – and ships – and sealing wax –
of CABBAGES – and kings –
And why the sea is boiling hot –
And whether pigs have wings.'

TWEEDLEDEE
Lewis Carroll

Red Cabbage & Apples

6 slices bacon
1 onion, chopped
¼ green pepper, cut in small strips
2 tart apples, sliced thinly
2 pounds red cabbage, shredded
2 tablespoons sugar
¼ teaspoon nutmeg
⅛ teaspoon black pepper
¼ teaspoon salt
¼ cup water
¼ cup dry red wine
2 tablespoons cider vinegar

Fry bacon in skillet to render drippings on medium heat. Remove bacon and cook onion and green pepper for 2 - 3 minutes. Stir in the cabbage and apples. Cover skillet and reduce heat; cook 2 - 3 minutes. Stir in sugar, nutmeg, black pepper and salt. Combine water, wine and vinegar; pour over cabbage. Cover skillet; simmer 15 - 20 minutes. Serve hot or cold.
Yield: 6 - 8 servings

Indicated Delicious New Potatoes

1 dozen small new potatoes, cleaned and scraped
1 teaspoon salt
2 tablespoons Crab and Shrimp Boil

Cover the potatoes with cold water and bring to a boil. Add salt and crab and shrimp boil. Boil until tender. Drain off water. Drain completely on paper towels. Pour cream sauce over top and serve. Serves: 6

Cream Sauce:

2 tablespoons butter
2 tablespoons flour, all-purpose
1 cup milk
½ teaspoon salt
dash white pepper
1 tablespoon parsley
1 teaspoon dry sherry

Melt butter, stir in flour and slowly add milk. Add salt and white pepper. Add parsley and cook on medium-low heat until thickened. Remove from heat and stir in sherry. Serve hot. Yield: 6 servings

"Let the sky rain potatoes."
THE MERRY WIVES OF WINDSOR
William Shakespeare

Mean Sea Parsleyed Peas

1 16-ounce package frozen green peas
4 tablespoons butter
½ teaspoon salt
1½ cups parsley, chopped finely

Prepare green peas according to package directions. Drain and set aside. In small saucepan melt butter on low heat and cook to golden brown. Add salt and parsley (do not stir). Cover and remove from heat; let stand 5 minutes. Toss peas with parsley mixutre gently. Serve immediately. Yield: 6 servings

"I always eat peas with honey
I've done it all my life,
They do taste kind of funny,
But it keeps them on the knife."

PEAS
Dr. Temple, Headmaster of Rugby

Steamed Broccoli with Sauce

1 large fresh broccoli, trimmed
2 tablespoons mayonnaise
1 tablespoon prepared mustard
1 tablespoon fresh lemon juice

Steam broccoli until just tender in a vegetable steamer. Remove immediately and add sauce over top. Yield: 4 servings

Sauce:

Whisk mayonnaise, mustard and lemon juice until just blended. Keep chilled until ready to serve.

Champion Creamed Spinach

3 packages fresh spinach, washed and drained
1 stick butter, unsalted
3 tablespoons flour, all-purpose
½ pint whipping cream
½ teaspoon salt
¼ teaspoon nutmeg
¼ teaspoon white pepper

Remove stems from spinach, wash and rinse three times. In large pot or steamer heat 6 cups water; bring to a boil and add a few sprinkles of salt. Place cleaned spinach in boiling water. Mash beneath the water with wooden spoon. Boil 3 - 5 minutes (do not overcook). Pour spinach into a colander, drain and rinse with cold water. Squeeze spinach one handful at a time to remove water. Cut spinach to chop. Place spinach in heavy saucepan and cook on medium heat to remove excess water while stirring. Add butter, melt and blend. Gradually add the flour; stir to blend. Gradually add the cream, stirring to blend. Reduce to low heat, cover and cook 5 - 7 minutes. Check and stir to prevent sticking. Add more cream if necessary. Stir in seasonings. Serve hot. Serves: 6 "This is wonderful for breakfast with scrambled eggs."

"The camel's hump is an ugly lump
Which well you may see at the Zoo;
But uglier yet is the hump we get
From having too little to do."

Rudyard Kipling

Unidentified Rice

1 cup onion, chopped
¼ cup butter
3 cups freshly cooked rice
2 cups sour cream
1 cup cottage cheese
1 large bay leaf
parsley and black pepper to taste
½ teaspoon salt
3 4-ounce cans whole green chiles, seeded and
    drained
2 cups sharp cheddar cheese, grated

Saute onion in butter until tender. Do not brown. Add cooked rice, sour cream, cottage cheese and bay leaf. Mix well and check for seasoning. Add parsley and black pepper to taste and salt. Mix and toss well. In a 4 quart buttered baking dish layer rice mixture, green chiles and cheese. Repeat layers ending with cheese on top. Bake uncovered 25 minutes at 375 degrees. Serves: 8 "Delicious hot or cold."

"MY FAVORITE"

Glazed Comet Carrots

10 fresh thin carrots, peeled and sliced
2 tablespoons butter
1 teaspoon sugar
¼ cup dry vermouth
1 tablespoon parsley, chopped

In a small skillet boil carrots in lightly salted water for 5 minutes until barely tender; drain and rinse with cold water. Melt butter in skillet, add carrots; sprinkle with sugar and saute 5 minutes. Stir in vermouth, cover partially and simmer 5 minutes. Add parsley, cover and let stand 3 minutes. Serves: 6

Crop Duster Corn Pudding

2 eggs
⅓ cup milk
2 cups cracker crumbs
1 16½-ounce can cream corn
4 tablespoons butter, melted
1 large carrot, sliced
½ cup green pepper, chopped
⅓ cup celery, chopped
⅓ cup onion, chopped
3 drops hot sauce
1 teaspoon sugar
½ teaspoon salt
1 teaspoon parsley
1 cup sharp cheddar cheese, shredded

Combine eggs and milk and beat well. Add cracker crumbs; set aside. Add remaining ingredients except cheese to crumb mixture. Stir well and spoon into a 2 quart baking dish. Bake at 350 degrees for 35 minutes (covered). Remove and sprinkle with cheese while hot. Serve immediately. Serves: 4 - 6

Top Rudder Ratatouille

2 onions, sliced
2 medium eggplants, cut into 1½ inch cubes
3 medium zucchini, sliced thickly
1 green pepper, seeded and cut in chunks
1 sweet red pepper, seeded and cut in chunks
2 small tomatoes, cut in chunks
1 tablespoon minced garlic
½ cup olive oil
3 tablespoons tomato paste
2 teaspoons salt
2 teaspoons basil
1 teaspoon oregano
2 tablespoons parsley, chopped finely
black pepper to taste

Layer the onions, eggplant, zucchini, peppers and tomatoes in a 6 quart baking dish. Combine garlic, olive oil, tomato paste, salt, basil, oregano, parsley and black pepper; mix well and pour over layers. Cover and bake at 350 degrees for 2 hours. Remove cover and bake 30 minutes to reduce liquid. Taste for seasoning and adjust accordingly. Serve hot or at room temperature.
Serves: 8 - 10

Certified Rice

2 cups water, hot
1 teaspoon salt
1 cup popcorn rice

Bring water to boil in heavy pot, add salt and popcorn rice. Stir twice. Place on cover. Reduce to simmer for 25 minutes. Remove from heat. Keep covered until ready to serve hot. "Popcorn rice is grown in Louisiana. It smells like popcorn while being cooked and has a slight corn taste."

Hopkins' Boarding House's Sweet Potato Souffle

4 cups mashed sweet potatoes (if potatoes are dry,
    add up to ½ cup evaporated milk)
½ cup sugar
½ cup butter or oleo
½ cup coconut
⅓ cup raisins
1 teaspoon lemon extract or orange peel
miniature marshmallows

1. While potatoes are hot, add all other ingredients.
2. Place in casserole dish. Cover with marshmallows.
3. Bake in 300 degree oven until marshmallows are brown, 20 - 30 minutes.

Serves: 6
Preparation: 10 minutes
Cooking: 30 minutes

"A nice accompaniment with smoked ham and perky green vegetables!"

THE HOPKINS' HOUSE, INC.
900 N. Spring Street
Pensacola, Florida 32501
438-3979

Stir-fried Asparagus

1 pound fresh asparagus, thin
1 tablespoon butter
1½ tablespoons vegetable oil
1 tablespoon fresh lemon juice
1 tablespoon water
salt and pepper to taste

Gently wash the asparagus well. Remove the coarse bottoms. Cut tender asparagus in ½ inch slices. Combine butter and oil in a skillet; heat at medium high heat. Add the asparagus and saute; tossing gently and frequently (about 2 minutes). Combine lemon juice and water; add to asparagus and cover. Reduce heat to medium and cook 3 minutes until just tender. Add salt and pepper to taste. Serve immediately. Yield: 6 - 8. "Asparagus will be crisp and 'flashing green'."

Creamed Cabbage Casserole

1 medium-head cabbage, finely shredded
¼ cup green pepper, chopped
½ cup boiling water, salted
3 tablespoons butter
3 tablespoons flour
½ teaspoon salt
¼ cup plain bread crumbs
¼ cup cheddar cheese, grated

Cook cabbage and green pepper in salted water for about 10 minutes (do not overcook). Drain. Place in a buttered 1½ quart casserole dish. Melt butter in saucepan, stir in flour and salt until smooth. Gradually add milk and continue stirring until thick. Pour sauce over cabbage and sprinkle with bread crumbs and cheese. Bake at 325 degrees for 15 minutes. "Delicious with fried corn bread." Serves: 4

No Wind Shear Baked Beans

1 pound ground chuck (necessary element to chuck shear)
½ pound bacon, cut into 3 inch pieces
1 rib celery, sliced
1½ cups onion, chopped
2 15-ounce cans pork and beans in tomato sauce, undrained
½ cup light brown sugar
1 teaspoon prepared mustard
1 12-ounce bottle chili sauce
½ teaspoon salt

Saute ground chuck, drain and set aside. Saute bacon to render drippings and saute celery and onion until soft. Combine chuck, bacon mixture, and all other ingredients in a 4 quart baking dish. Bake at 325 degrees for 2 hours uncovered. Stir each 30 minutes. Serve hot or at room temperature. Serves: 8

Easy RUN-UP Vegetable Quiche

1 10-ounce package frozen broccoli
2 teaspoons olive oil
1 cup onions, chopped
½ cup green peppers, chopped
1 clove garlic, minced
1 3-ounce can mushrooms, sliced
3 fresh tomatoes, peeled and chopped
6 eggs, beaten
½ teaspoon basil
1 teaspoon oregano
1 tablespoon parsley
1 teaspoon salt
black pepper to taste
3 tablespoons tomato paste
½ cup Parmesan cheese, grated
1 cup Swiss cheese, grated
12 black olives, sliced

Prepare broccoli according to package directions, drain and set aside. Heat olive oil in heavy skillet and add onions, green pepper, garlic and mushrooms. Saute 6 minutes. Add tomatoes and cook to remove liquid. (Use low heat.) Add broccoli to skillet. In mixing bowl combine eggs, basil, oregano, parsley, salt, black pepper to taste, and tomato paste. Mix with beater to blend tomato paste. Stir in cheeses. Combine egg mixture with cooked vegetables. Pour into baking dish over fillo pastry. Top with olives. Bake at 350 degrees for 30 minutes. Serve hot or at room temperature. Serves: 6 - 8

Note: Fresh steamed broccoli may be substituted.

Continued on next page →

Easy RUN-UP Vegetable Quiche (Continued)

Fillo pastry crust:

4 leaves fillo
½ cup bread crumbs or fillo flakes
½ stick butter, melted

Place 4 leaves fillo pastry in a buttered 9 x 13 inch baking dish; buttering after each layer and sprinkle bread crumbs or fillo flakes after each layer.

The Wright Rice

¾ stick butter, melted
1 6-ounce can mushroom pieces
1 10½-ounce can onion soup
1 small can water chestnuts, sliced and drained
1 cup raw rice
1 soup can water
salt and pepper to taste

Combine all ingredients in covered baking dish. Bake at 350 degrees for 1 hour. Stir with fork after 30 minutes. Serve immediately. Serves: 6

Hopkins' Boarding House's Fried Squash

2 pounds yellow squash (may substitute zucchini)
salt
self-rising flour
fat for deep fat frying

1. Wash and slice squash into 1 inch pieces.
2. Sprinkle salt over squash so that all pieces are lightly salted. (The salt draws out the extra liquid)
3. Let stand 1 hour. Pour off liquid.
4. Dip and completely cover each piece in self-rising flour.
5. Fry in deep fat at 350 degrees until brown and crisp.

Serves: 6
Preparation: 1 hour 15 minutes
Cooking: 10 minutes

"A nice change for an old favorite!"

THE HOPKINS' HOUSE, INC.
900 N. Spring Street
Pensacola, Florida 32501
438-3979

Asparagus Blade Tips

2 pounds fresh asparagus, tender tips only
¼ stick butter
⅓ cup sesame seeds
¼ cup fresh lemon juice
salt to taste

In vegetable steamer, steam asparagus 8 - 10 minutes. Do not overcook. In saucepan heat butter and saute sesame seeds until golden. Add lemon juice and heat. Place asparagus on serving dish and pour over sauce. Salt to taste. Yield: 8 servings

Beans and Rice

1 pound pinto beans, dry
½ cup onion, chopped
½ cup chili powder
1 teaspoon crushed red pepper
½ teaspoon salt
dash garlic salt
dash sugar
smoked sausage
ham pieces

In 3 quart stock pot add dry beans and 2 quarts water. Add all other ingredients now, except the sausage and ham. Cook this mixture on medium heat for about 2½ to 3 hours, covered. Add smoked sausage and ham to cooked beans and cook this mixture another 30 minutes. Serve hot over white rice, with garlic bread.

Note: "These are absolutely delicious!" We used hot sausage and reduced the chili powder to ⅓ cup.

LEON'S on Monkhouse Drive is ideal for lunch. It is less than 5 minutes from Shreveport Regional Airport.

Leon's
SMOKED TURKEY

4723 Monkhouse Drive
Shreveport, LA 71109
(318) 635-5700
Also East Kings Highway Location

Echo Eggplant

2 eggplants, peeled and sliced into ¼ inch slices
2 eggs, beaten
2 cups Italian bread crumbs
¼ cup Romano cheese, grated
¼ cup Parmesan cheese, grated
¼ cup dried parsley
1 teaspoon salt
¼ teaspoon black pepper
1 teaspoon garlic powder
olive oil
1 16-ounce can stewed tomatoes
½ teaspoon dried basil
½ teaspoon oregano

Dip eggplant slices into beaten eggs. Combine bread crumbs, Romano cheese, Parmesan cheese, parsley, salt, pepper and garlic powder. Dredge the egg coated eggplant slices in bread crumb mixture. Saute eggplant slices in hot olive oil until brown. Drain on paper towels. (May be served hot at this point or continue.) Layer eggplant slices in a baking casserole with stewed tomatoes. Sprinkle with basil, oregano, additional bread crumbs and Parmesan cheese. Bake at 350 degrees for 15 - 20 minutes. Serve immediately. Serves: 6

Note: Eggplant may be cut in sticks ¼ inch thick if desired. When fried as above, they are delicious served with butter.

Sunbeam Sweet Potato Casserole

8 sweet potatoes
1 cup milk, scalded
½ stick butter, melted
3 tablespoons sugar
1 teaspoon vanilla extract
¼ teaspoon cinnamon
¼ teaspoon nutmeg
1 tablespoon orange juice
marshmallows

Bake sweet potatoes at 350 degrees until tender (about 30 minutes). Peel hot potatoes and put through a ricer to remove strings. Using electric mixer combine sweet potatoes with scalded milk, butter, and sugar. Mix well. Add vanilla, cinnamon, nutmeg and orange juice. Place ½ mixture in a buttered baking dish. Layer marshmallows. Continue with potato mixture and top with marshmallows. Bake at 350 degrees until top layer of marshmallows is brown and melted (about 20 minutes). Serves: 6
"Absolutely delicious, but requires time and effort. We always have this for Thanksgiving dinner. Watch carefully in the oven. Once, we did have to use the Hallon!" As J. B. says, "You always know when Marlene is in the kitchen, you either see smoke or blood!"

Homestead, Braddock, Birmingham,
they make their steel with men,
smoke and blood is the mix of
steel.

SMOKE AND STEEL
Carl Sandburg, 1878

– *Notes* –

MEATS AND POULTRY

*The winter evening settles down
with smell of steaks in
passageways.*

THE MYSTERY CAT
Thomas Stearns Eliot, 1888-1965

Chicken Wellington
for that Special Dinner Party

2 whole chicken breasts, skinned, boned, halved,
    excess fat removed, flattened
2 Pepperidge Farm Patty shells, thawed
    (Available at most markets.)
1 small can of pate, or fresh pate from a specialty
    market
2 large mushrooms without stems
sprig of chopped parsley
½ cup flavored bread crumbs
2 teaspoons olive oil
2 teaspoons water
flour for rolling patty shells
1 egg
½ teaspoon milk

Red Rooster Tavern

7385 Post Road
North Kingston,
Rhode Island 02852
(401) 295-8804

1. In a flat dish, press crumbs into chicken on both sides.
2. In a saute pan using half the oil, lightly saute the breaded chicken breasts. (Reserve and cool.)
3. On a floured board, roll thawed patty shells about 8 x 8 round. (Reserve and keep cool.)

Assembly

1. On a flat surface, lay out pastry, top successively with one cooked chicken breast, slice of pate, other chicken breast, add more pate, parsley, top with mushroom cap.
2. Do this with each portion.
3. Wrap chicken like a package, sealing seams with water.
4. In a cup beat egg and milk with a fork.
5. Spread egg mixture on crust with fingers or pastry brush.
6. Put chicken on oiled and floured cookie sheet.
7. Bake on top shelf of preheated 425 degree oven for 20 minutes.
8. Remove from oven with a pancake turner.

Sunshine Chicken

8 chicken breast fillets, cut in 2 inch strips
1 lemon
1 recipe Seasoned Batter
vegetable oil, 3 inches or more

Place chicken in shallow bowl or pan and squeeze the juice of 1 lemon over the top. Marinate 15 minutes to refresh and season. Drain and pat dry thoroughly with paper towels. In a large bowl coat chicken completely with seasoned batter. Submerge one chicken slice at a time into preheated electric deep-fat fryer (360 degrees). Add carefully and slowly. Use tongs or long fork to move about gently. Deep fry 7 - 12 minutes until golden brown. Remove and drain on paper towels. It will be necessary to cook several batches (4 - 5 pieces at a time). "Delicious crunchy crust." Serves: 4 - 6

Seasoned Batter:

> 1 cup flour, all-purpose
> 1 teaspoon salt
> ½ teaspoon paprika
> ½ teaspoon black pepper
> ½ teaspoon red pepper
> ¼ teaspoon oregano
> 1 egg
> 1 tablespoon butter, melted
> ½ cup beer

Combine dry ingredients in a large mixing bowl. In a small bowl beat the egg with melted butter and add beer. Stir beer mixture into dry ingredients until blended. Add chicken pieces one at a time to coat well. "This batter is also delicious for vegetables and seafood."

Curry For The Crew

1½ cups water
4 bay leaves
1 stick whole cinnamon
5 whole cloves
½ cup vegetable oil
2 large green peppers, chopped finely
2 cloves garlic, minced
4 medium onions, chopped finely
2 large fresh ripe tomatoes, chopped
1½ teaspoons salt
½ teaspoon turmeric
1 teaspoon white pepper
1 teaspoon ground cumin
1 teaspoon coriander
1 tablespoon paprika
2 tablespoons curry powder
5 pounds boneless chicken pieces, deskinned
3 tablespoons flour

In a small saucepan combine water, bay leaves, cinnamon and cloves; bring to a boil and simmer for ½ hour. Heat the oil in a deep skillet. Add green peppers, garlic and onions; cook on medium heat until tender and lightly browned. Add tomatoes, salt, turmeric, white pepper, cumin, coriander, paprika and curry powder. Stir and simmer covered for 15 minutes. Dust chicken pieces lightly with flour and place on top of the skillet mixture. Pour the water from the boiled spices over the chicken. Cover and simmer until chicken is tender (about 1 hour). Serve hot with a variety of condiments. Suggestions: Hot raisin rice, mango chutney, pineapple pickles, chopped boiled egg, coconut flakes, sliced bananas with yogurt cream, golden raisins, or diced apple with yogurt cream. Serves: 8

Note: Lamb, beef or shrimp may be substituted for chicken.

Roast Veal Shank

2 3½-pound milk-fed veal shanks
salt
pepper
1 cup diced celery
1 cup diced carrots
1 cup diced onions
2 cups beef or meat stock or bouillon
1 cup packed julienned carrots (about 2 medium
    carrots)
1 cup packed julienned zucchini (about 1 medium
    zucchini)
1 cup packed julienned onion (about 1 medium
    onion)
1 cup packed julienned cauliflower florets
24 small whole mushrooms
½ stick butter
salt to taste
black pepper to taste

Rub the veal shanks thoroughly with salt and pepper. Place the shanks in a roasting pan, and place the pan in a 450-degree oven. Roast the shanks uncovered for ½ hour. Add the diced celery, carrots, and onions to the pan, and pour in 1 cup of the stock. Cover the pan, and cook the shanks at 300 degrees for another ½ hour. Remove the pan from the oven. Add the second cup of stock, and baste the shanks with the pan juices. Return the shanks, uncovered, to the oven, and cook them for approximately 1½ hours, basting every ½ hour.

Remove the shanks from pan. Strain the juices and vegetables from roasting pan, reserving the juices and discarding the vegetables. Remove the fat as it rises to the top of the strained juices.

In a large frying pan, stir-fry or pan-saute' the julienned carrots, zucchini, onion, cauliflower, and the mushrooms in the butter for

Continued on next page →

Roast Veal Shank (Continued)

4-5 minutes over medium high heat. The vegetables should be served al dente or crispy. Add salt and pepper to taste, and serve the vegetables over the warmed veal shanks. Serve the juice on the side. Serves: 6

Creative European Cuisine

WILLY COLN'S CHALET
2505 Whitney Avenue
Gretna, Louisiana 70053
361-3860

WILLY COLN'S
  KALEIDOSCOPE
Canal Place – 3rd Level
New Orleans, LA 70130

Perfect Pattern Pork Chops

8 pork chops, 1½ inch thick
salt and black pepper to taste
2 tablespoons vegetable oil
½ cup damson preserves*
2 tablespoons hot sweet mustard*
½ cup white wine vinegar

Season chops with salt and black pepper. In a large nonstick skillet brown the chops on both sides. Combine the preserves and mustard; blend. Spread the mixture over the chops evenly. Cover the skillet and simmer chops 45 minutes. Remove chops to heated platter and keep warm. Chill skillet slightly in refrigerator to aid in removing excess fat from pan drippings. Return skillet to medium heat and bring to a boil. Add vinegar, stir and blend with juices and brown bits. Boil to reduce slightly. Pour over chops and serve immediately. Yield: 8

*(See index)

CockPIT Barbecued Brisket

1 12-ounce can beer
6 cups water
1 onion, sliced
2 cloves garlic, minced
1 6-pound beef brisket
CockPIT Barbecue Sauce* (See Below)

Combine all ingredients except the sauce in a large heavy skillet. Bring to a boil; reduce heat and simmer covered until tender (about 4 hours). Allow to cool in liquids until lukewarm. Place brisket in a plastic bag and add 2 cups CockPit barbecue sauce. Refrigerate for 48 hours. Remove excess sauce from brisket and let stand 1 hour to reduce chill. Cook over hot coals 15 minutes each side and baste with fresh CockPit barbecue sauce. Slice and serve hot or cold with additional sauce. Serves: 18 - 20

*(See index)   *"Let's carve him as a dish fit for the gods."*
BRUTUS

Soaring Sweet and Sour Chicken Wings

3 pounds small chicken legs, wing part
1 cup lemon juice
¼ cup sugar
½ cup light brown sugar
2½ tablespoons cornstarch
1 teaspoon salt
½ teaspoon ground ginger
¼ teaspoon black pepper
1 cup chicken broth
¼ cup soy sauce

Clean and refresh chicken with ½ cup lemon juice for bath. Place chicken in baking dish. Combine remaining ½ cup lemon juice and all other ingredients; pour over the chicken. Bake at 350 degrees for 1 hour uncovered. Serve immediately or at room temperature. Serves: 4 - 6

HOLDING SHORT Ribs of Beef

    4 pounds lean short ribs of beef, cut in 3 inch
        pieces
    2 large onions, sliced
    1 large carrot, sliced
    8 celery ribs with leaves
    ¼ cup vegetable oil

Place beef, 1 onion, carrot and celery in a heavy skillet; cover with
water and bring to a boil. Cover and simmer until the meat is
tender (about 3 hours). Remove the beef, strain and degrease the
stock. In a skillet add oil, 1 onion and beef. Brown beef and onion
in hot oil. Pour ½ gravy recipe over top and bake 45 minutes
uncovered until nicely browned. Serve hot with gravy.
Serves: 4 - 6

Gravy:

    ¼ cup vegetable oil
    ¼ cup flour, all-purpose
    3 cups stock (or less)
    salt and pepper to taste
    ½ teaspoon marjoram
    ½ teaspoon brown coloring

In skillet heat oil and blend in flour. Gradually stir in stock. Cook
and stir until gravy boils 1 minute. Add salt and pepper to taste.
Add majoram and food coloring. Stir. Serve hot.

*Sir Humphry Davy
Detested gravy.
He lived in the odium
of having discovered sodium.*

Edmund Clerihew Bentley, 1875-1956

CockPIT Barbecue Sauce

2 24-ounce bottles catsup
½ cup cider vinegar
2 tablespoons chili powder
¼ cup brown sugar
3 bay leaves
2 cups onions, chopped finely
½ cup worcestershire sauce
1 stick butter
6 garlic cloves, minced
½ teaspoon red pepper flakes
½ teaspoon liquid smoke
4½ cups beer

Combine all ingredients in a large skillet. Bring to a boil. Reduce heat, cover and simmer 1 hour. Remove bay leaves. Refrigerate sauce 8 hours in covered container before using. Yield: 10 cups. Sauce retains flavor and freshness for 1 month if refrigerated.

"Delicious on brisket, chicken, ribs or chops."

Philip's Supper House Chicken Angelo

3 whole chicken breasts
flour
clarified butter
dash oregano
dash basil
salt, pepper
⅓ cup dry white wine
½ to 1 small lemon
2 cloves garlic, minced
1 cup sliced mushrooms
6 quartered canned or frozen artichoke hearts
1 tablespoon chopped parsley
2 tablespoons brandy

Have chicken breasts boned and cut into 12 pieces. Dredge in flour. Shake off excess flour. Heat ¼ cup clarified butter in large skillet over medium heat. When hot, add chicken pieces and brown on all sides. Add oregano, basil and season with salt and pepper to taste. Add 2 tablespoons clarified butter to skillet. Heat, then add wine, lemon juice and garlic. Reduce heat and saute 4 to 5 minutes. Add sliced mushrooms, artichoke hearts and parsley. Saute until mushrooms are tender, about 3 minutes. Turn to high heat and add brandy. Heat and ignite. Let flames die down. Serve at once. Makes 6 servings.

4545 West Sahara Avenue
Las Vegas, Nevada 89102
(702) 873-5222

I AIM to cook Perfect Meat Loaf

2 cups onion, minced
2 tablespoons butter
1 cup fresh white bread crumbs
2 pounds lean ground beef
1 pound fresh ground pork
½ cup beef bouillon
2 eggs, beaten
⅔ cup sharp cheddar cheese, grated
1 tablespoon salt
½ teaspoon black pepper
1 teaspoon oregano
½ teaspoon all spice
3 bay leaves

Saute onions in butter until clear and tender. Mix well with remaining ingredients reserving the bay leaves. Form and shape into a loaf; place in a buttered loaf pan. Place the bay leaves on top. Bake at 350 degrees for 2 hours. Cool 30 minutes. Pour off any excess drippings. Serve hot or wrap in foil and chill for picnic. Yield: 1 large loaf

Veal Elizabeth

1 5-ounce veal
4 ounces butter
1 tablespoon shallots, chopped
3 tablespoons white wine
4 tablespoons Mader Wine
½ cup cream
4 ounces white sauce
salt and pepper
2 asparagus
2 broccoli spears
½ ounce Languini with garlic sauce

Saute veal until golden brown.
Remove veal from pan, put ½ ounce of butter, saute shallots until golden brown, put white wine and Mader wine, reduce heat for 3 minutes. Put in cream and reduce again for 2 minutes. Put in white sauce and let boil for 3 - 4 minutes.
Saute the vegetables on side with butter. Cook languini. Put garlic sauce and salt and pepper to taste.
Put veal on plate, put aspargus on the veal, broccoli spears on side with languini and top with sauce. Serve hot. Serves: 1

By CHEF BONETTI, CEC.

THE RENAISSANCE

The Cornhusker
333 South 13th Street • Lincoln, Nebraska 68508 • (402) 474-7474

Threshold Bounty Breast of Chicken

4 whole chicken breasts, boned and skinned
2 tablespoons flour
¼ cup butter
1 3-ounce can mushrooms, sliced
1 10½-ounce can beef consomme
½ cup sour cream
1 teaspoon salt
¼ teaspoon black pepper
1 tablespoon parmesan cheese, grated

Sprinkle chicken with flour and saute in butter until lightly browned. Add mushrooms and consomme; cover and simmer for 45 minutes. Stir in sour cream, salt, pepper and cheese. Simmer uncovered 10 minutes (do not boil). Serves: 4

At a dinner party one
should eat wisely but not too well,
and talk well but not too wisely.

W. SOMERSET MAUGHAM

Peppered Tournedos Grand Marnier

4 filet mignons, sliced in half
1 tablespoon chopped shallots
2 juice oranges, peeled, membrane removed, and
    cut into segments
4 teaspoons green peppercorns (in brine), drained
2 ounces Grand Marnier
2 ounces brandy
12 ounces veal demi-glace (reduced veal stock)
4 tablespoons clarified, unsalted butter
2 teaspoons whole, unsalted butter

Sear tournedos in hot clarified butter. Remove and keep warm.
Add shallots to pan, then orange segments and green peppercorns. Deglaze with Grand Marnier, then brandy. Add veal
demi-glace. Add salt and pepper to taste. Remove pan from heat
and wisk in whole butter to finish sauce.
To serve, place tournedos side by side on each of the warmed
plates. Spoon finished sauce over the meat. Garnish tops with
orange segments. Serve with a bouquetier of vegetables and
potato croquettes. Serves: 4

Corner of Marlborough and Farewell Streets
Newport, Rhode Island 02840
849-3600

HOVER Ham

1 medium boneless ham
water
1 large orange
1 bag crab boil seasoning

Place ham in a large skillet; add water to cover. Squeeze orange to render juice. Thickly slice the orange peeling. Add juice and peeling slices to ham. Place seasoning bag unopened in the water beside ham. Bring to a boil; cover and simmer 3 hours. Remove immediately from cooking liquids. Slice and serve hot or cold or further process with glaze. Serves: 6

Glaze:

¼ cup Madeira
⅓ cup light brown sugar
1 cup prepared mustard

Combine ingredients and smooth over top of ham. Bake at 350 degrees for 30 minutes, basting frequently with glaze. Remove and let stand before slicing.

Aviator Veal Marsala

2 pounds veal steak, cut into 1½ inch strips
salt and white pepper to taste
1 egg
½ cup heavy cream
2 tablespoons flour
3 tablespoons olive oil
3 tablespoons butter, unsalted
½ pound fresh mushrooms
1 large green pepper, seeded and cut into 1 inch
    strips
1 cup chicken broth
½ cup dry Florio Marsala wine
spaghetti

Place veal between pieces of waxpaper; beat and flatten thin
(about ⅛ inch). Season with salt and pepper. In a small bowl beat
the egg and cream. Dip veal in egg mixture and then into flour.
Heat oil and butter in a large skillet. Saute veal until brown
turning only once (3-4 minutes); remove veal and lightly brown
mushrooms; add green pepper; stir and cook 1 minute. Return
veal to skillet; add broth with ¼ cup of the wine. Cover and
simmer 45 minutes. Remove from heat; stir in the remaining
wine. Serve over hot spaghetti. Serves: 4

– *Notes* –

FISH and SHELLFISH

"I sent a message to the fish: I told them 'this is what I wish!"

Humpty Dumpty
THROUGH THE LOOKING GLASS
Lewis Carroll

Baked Flying Fish

6 flying fish, cleaned and deboned
1 teaspoon salt
juice of 2 lemons
2 tablespoons seasoning (below)
1 teaspoon prepared mustard
1 tablespoon flour
2 tablespoons butter, melted
1 teaspoon vinegar
1 cup water
1 tomato, sliced thinly
2 onions, sliced thinly
lemon garnish

*"On the road to Mandalay
where the flyin'-fishes play."*
Rudyard Kipling, 1865-1936

Sprinkle fish with salt and lemon juice; marinate for 15 minutes. Prepare seasoning (below). Rinse fish, pat dry with paper towels and season with seasoning. Start at the tail and roll the fish forward; securing with picks. Place the rolled fish in a baking dish or pan. Combine and add mustard, flour, butter, vinegar, water, tomato and sliced onion. Cover and bake at 400 degrees for 20 minutes. Garnish with lemon. Serves: 6

Seasoning:

¼ teaspoon cloves
¼ teaspoon thyme
1 clove garlic, minced
dash red pepper
½ teaspoon salt

1 medium onion, chopped finely
¼ cup chives, chopped
1 teaspoon lemon juice

Combine all ingredients and blend well.

"It is very likely that you would have an occasion to cook a flying fish. It is considered a delicacy in the Caribbean and Japan. They have also been reported flying off the coast of Louisiana and Florida. If you are fishing in these waters, you might try fishing at night as the flying fish are attracted to lights. Use a flash light or lantern on your boat or seaplane as a beacon. The flying fish have been known to land right on the deck."

Red Snapper En Papillote

4 fillets red snapper
24 bay scallops
4 large shrimp, deveined and butterflied
24 mussels, scrubbed, remaining closed
Garlic marinara, recipe follows
Cafe de Paris sauce, recipe follows

Preheat oven to 350 degrees. Lay out 4 large pieces of aluminum foil, each about 18-inches square. Lay 1 fillet on each piece of foil. Arrange a quarter of the scallops, shrimp and mussels around each fish. Divide the garlic marinara in 4 portions and cover each fish with 1 portion. Place 1 tablespoon of Cafe de Paris sauce over the garlic marinara. Fold foil over, leaving plenty of air space. Seal the edges tightly.

Place on individual oven platters and cook in oven for 12 minutes. Place platter on second platter for serving at the table. Slit foil crosswise to open. Fold back to make eating easy. Serves: 4

Garlic Marinara

1 can (8-ounce) Italian plum tomatoes
2 cloves garlic, crushed
2 tablespoons olive oil
2 pinches oregano
1 teaspoon chopped parsley

Drain tomatoes and chop. Saute garlic with olive oil for 1 minute or until golden. Remove garlic and add tomatoes to the pan. Saute for 4 minutes. Add oregano and parsley. Saute for 1 minute more. Make sure the Garlic Marinara is very thick. If it is too runny the liquid from the mussels will make this dish too watery.

Continued on next page →

Red Snapper En Papillote (Continued)

Cafe de Paris Sauce

4 tablespoons butter, softened
2 teaspoons minced garlic
2 teaspoons minced parsley
1 shallot, minced
Pinch of nutmeg
1 tablespoon grated orange skin
1 teaspoon Pernod
1 tablespoon lemon juice
Salt and pepper to taste

The Captain's Table

Musso's 860-2 Rest., Inc.

Sea Foods and Continental Specialties

860 Second Avenue - Corner 46th Street
New York, New York 10017-Phone: (212) 697-9538

Lightening Flash Fish with cream sauce

4 - 6 fresh trout fillets
½ teaspoon salt
¼ teaspoon white pepper
½ teaspoon dried dill
3 tablespoons flour, all-purpose
½ stick unsalted butter
1½ cups heavy cream

Sprinkle trout with salt, pepper and dill. Dredge with flour. Saute in hot butter until golden brown on both sides (turning only once). Add cream to saucepan pouring over the trout. Cover and simmer 3 - 4 minutes to slightly reduce liquid. Serve hot with certified rice. Serves 4 - 6

"Glory be to God for
dappled things -
For skies of couple-colour
as a brinded cow;
For rose-moles All in
stipple upon Trout
that swim."

PIED BEAUTY
Gerard Manley Hopkins, 1844-1889

Abalone La Brasserie

Step 1 – Place abalone on slightly damp wooden board. Gently pound abalone with light hammer . . . **both sides.**

Step 2 – Make an egg batter . . . whipping 2 or 3 eggs until liquified.

Step 3 – Lightly coat abalone with flour (season flour with salt and pepper to taste) and dip into egg batter.

Step 4 – Take 2 skillets. Lightly oil skillet #1 and put on fire. When oil is very hot (before smoking) place abalone in same, cooking not more than 5 seconds per side. Remove abalone from skillet and place on hot plates. Take skillet #2 and put

> **2 tablespoons of butter**
> **1 teaspoonful of lemon juice**
> **½ ounce of white wine**
> **and capers to taste**

Slowly heat and blend the foregoing. When all the ingredients are liquified pour over the abalone and add croutons. Serve hot.

LA BRASSERIE
202 South Main Street
Orange, California

"Lake" Trout

4 - 6 fresh trout fillets
½ teaspoon salt
¼ teaspoon white pepper
¼ teaspoon paprika
¼ teaspoon nutmeg
3 tablespoons flour
½ stick butter, unsalted

Sprinkle seasonings on trout and dredge with flour. Saute until golden brown in hot butter. Serve with saute almonds and fresh lemon if desired. Serves: 4 - 6

Trout, Out of the Blue

4 - 6 fresh trout fillets
4 tablespoons worcestershire sauce
4 tablespoons fresh lemon juice
3 tablespoons flour
½ stick butter, unsalted

Place trout in shallow container flat and separated. Sprinkle with worcestershire sauce and lemon juice. Allow to rest 10 - 15 minutes. Remove one fillet at a time to dredge with flour and place in hot butter. Reserve the worcestershire - lemon mixture. Saute trout until golden brown (turning only once). Remove trout and reduce heat to simmer. Add worcestershire - lemon mixture to saucepan and simmer 1 - 2 minutes. Pour sauce over trout. Serve hot. Serves: 4 - 6

"Fish hold the honors for
being brain producers, even
though they haven't done as well as
they might with their own organism."

C. C. & F. M. Furnas

Gulf Stream Shrimp Barbecued

1½ pounds butter
½ teaspoon salt
red pepper, several dashes
juice of ½ lemon
1 teaspoon garlic powder
6 peppercorns
2 tablespoons black pepper
2 shakes hot sauce
3 tablespoons Worcestershire sauce
4 pounds fresh shrimp

Remove heads from shrimp and rinse well. In large shallow baking pan melt butter and add seasonings. Place shrimp in sauce and lightly toss. Broil shrimp 3" from broiler until red and tender (about 15 minutes). Remove and turn several times while broiling. Serve hot with French bread for sauce. Place empty bowls for shells and lemon-flavored finger-tips or bowl for clean-up. Serves: 4 - 6. Left over shrimp may be peeled and used in salads.

Halibut in Wine Sauce

2 pounds halibut
2 tablespoons butter
2 tablespoons shallots, minced
½ pound fresh mushrooms, sliced
⅔ cup dry white wine

Place halibut in a shallow pan and dot with butter. Sprinkle with shallots and add salt and pepper to taste, top with mushrooms and pour wine over all. Cover pan with foil and bake in preheated oven at 325 degrees for 15 minutes. Serves: 6

LA BRASSERIE
202 South Main Street
Orange, California

Salmon Ring

2 cups bread crumbs, The Wright Bread* (3 slices)
⅓ cup milk
2 eggs, beaten
2 cups salmon, drained and flaked
1 cup onion, chopped finely
1 tablespoon fresh parsley, minced
½ teaspoon dried dill
10 black olives, chopped finely
½ teaspoon black pepper
1 dash hot sauce
¼ teaspoon dry mustard
2 tablespoons lemon juice

Combine bread crumbs, milk and eggs in small bowl; set aside. Combine and mix salmon with remaining ingredients; add bread crumb mixture. Mix well. Place in an 8 inch greased ring mold and bake at 400 degrees for 30 minutes. To serve fill ring with Dizzy Dill Sauce and stand whole green onions in the sauce.
Serves: 6 *This is good hot or cold."* *(See index)

Note: May also be prepared as a loaf.

Dizzy Dill Sauce
½ cup mayonnaise
1 tablespoon parsley
1 tablespoon dried dill
¼ teaspoon white pepper
1 dill pickle, chopped finely
2 tablespoons lemon juice
2 tablespoons buttermilk

Combine ingredients, blend and chill.

Philip's Supper House Blackened Whitefish

¾ pound (3 sticks) unsalted butter, melted in a
    skillet

Seasoning Mix:
    1 tablespoon sweet paprika
    2½ teaspoons salt
    1 teaspoon onion powder
    1 teaspoon garlic powder
    1 teaspoon ground red pepper, preferably cayenne
    ¾ teaspoon white pepper
    ¾ teaspoon black pepper
    ½ teaspoon dried thyme leaves
    ½ teaspoon dried oregano leaves
    6 (8 to 10 ounce) orange roughy fillets

Heat a large cast-iron skillet over very high heat until it is beyond the smoking stage and you see white ash in the skillet bottom (the skillet cannot be too hot for this dish), at least 10 minutes. Thoroughly combine the seasoning mix ingredients in a small bowl. Dip each fillet in the melted butter so that both sides are well coated; then sprinkle seasoning mix generously and evenly on both sides of the fillets, patting it by hand. Place in the hot skillet and pour 1 teaspoon melted butter on top of each fillet (be careful, as the butter may flame up). Cook, uncovered, over the same high heat until the underside looks charred, about 2 minutes (the time will vary according to the fillet's thickness and the heat of the skillet). Turn the fish over and again pour 1 teaspoon butter on top; cook until fish is done, about 2 minutes more. Repeat with remaining fillets. Serve each fillet while piping hot. Makes 6 servings.

PHILIPS SUPPER HOUSE
4545 West Sahara Avenue
Las Vegas, Nevada 89102
(702) 873-5222

Approach-a-plate Louisiana Shrimp

2 cups cooked certified rice
1 4-ounce can mushrooms, drained
2 tablespoons butter
1 10¾-ounce can cream of shrimp soup
1 cup sour cream
2 tablespoons dry sherry
½ teaspoon salt
1 4-ounce can whole green chilies, deseeded and
    chopped
1 small can sliced water chestnuts, optional
2½ - 3 pounds fresh shrimp, boiled and peeled
¾ cup sharp cheddar cheese, shredded

Prepare rice and spread a shallow layer in a buttered baking dish
(4 quart size). Saute mushrooms in butter until tender. Stir in
shrimp soup, sour cream, sherry, salt, chilies and water chestnuts.
Heat slowly while stirring gently. Do not boil. Stir in shrimp;
heating slowly. Spread a layer of the shrimp mixture over the rice
in the baking dish. Continue layers, ending with shrimp mixture.
Sprinkle cheese over top and cover. Bake 15 - 20 minutes at 350
degrees. Serve hot. Serves: 6 - 8

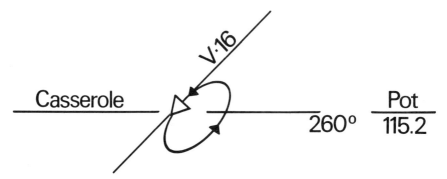

Hold north of Casserole, Left turns

Lobster with Basil and Cream

Court Bouillion:

> 8 quarts water
> 8 tablespoons Kosher salt
> 4 teaspoons crushed black peppercorns
> 2⅔ cups white vinegar
> Bouquet Garni

Sauce:

> 1½ teaspoons finely chopped basil
> 1½ teaspoons olive oil
> 5 cups heavy cream
> salt and pepper to taste
> raw diced tomatoes (garnish)

Boil court bouillion about 10 minutes. Cook 10 lobsters 14 minutes; remove and refrigerate.

Place cream in stainless steel pot. Bring to boil, reduce about 10 minutes, then, add basil mixed with olive oil. Salt and pepper to taste. Garnish with diced tomato. Sauce yield: approximately 12 to 14 orders.

Restaurant

5030 Centre Avenue
Pittsburgh, PA 15213
412/621-0744

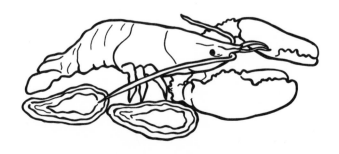

Aviator Crab Au Gratin

1 stick butter or margarine
1 teaspoon salt
½ teaspoon red pepper
¼ teaspoon white pepper
1 cup onion, finely chopped
1 stalk celery, finely chopped
½ cup flour, all-purpose
1⅔ cup milk, warm
2 egg yolks, beaten
1½ ounces dry white wine
1 pound white lump crabmeat
Parmesan cheese

Melt butter in large skillet on medium heat. Add salt, red pepper
and white pepper. Stir to blend and cook until butter is golden (2
minutes). Add onions and celery and cook until wilted. Reduce
heat and blend in flour well and gradually add milk, stirring
constantly to blend. Add egg yolks and cook for 5 minutes. In
large mixing bowl combine wine, crabmeat and flour mixture
gently. Pour into lightly buttered casserole (4 quart) and sprinkle
with cheese. Bake at 300 degrees for 15 minutes. Serve hot with
rice. Does not freeze well. Serves: 6 - 8

Shrimp Creole

6 slices bacon
3 tablespoons vegetable oil
¼ cup flour, all-purpose
2 cloves garlic, chopped
1 cup green pepper, chopped
2 cups onions, chopped
½ cup green onions (tops, too) chopped
1 cup celery, chopped (use tender heart)
2 fresh tomatoes, peeled and chopped
1 tablespoon salt
½ teaspoon black pepper
1½ teaspoons thyme
3 bay leaves
1 16-ounce can tomatoes, chopped
1 8-ounce can tomato sauce
1 6-ounce can tomato paste
1 cup fish stock (made from boiling shells)
3½ to 4 pounds peeled, deveined, raw shrimp
¼ cup dried parsley
1 teaspoon hot sauce
1 tablespoon lemon juice

In a large skillet fry bacon to render drippings. Combine drippings with vegetable oil and flour to make a dark brown roux. Cook on medium heat stirring constantly. Add garlic, green pepper, onions, celery, fresh tomatoes, salt, pepper, thyme and bay leaves. Stir and cook uncovered until onions are soft and clear. Add canned tomatoes, tomato sauce, tomato paste and stock; mix well. Cover and simmer for 1 hour. Add shrimp; adjust heat to medium high and cook for 5 - 7 minutes. Add parsley, hot sauce and lemon juice. Cover and remove from heat. Serve over rice, broiled Trout or Red Fish. This delicious dish freezes well. To reheat; heat quickly without boiling. Serves: 18

Fried Butterfly Shrimp

Shrimp (shelled and deveined)
1 egg, beaten
1 cup flour
½ teaspoon salt
½ teaspoon sugar
Vegetable oil, 3 inches or more

Butterfly the shrimp by lightly splitting up the back or outside curve with a kitchen knife. (Do not sever.) Pat shrimp dry with paper towel. Dip shrimp into egg and then dust with the flour and seasonings. Drop into preheated electric deep-fat fryer (360 degrees). Fry until golden brown (about 3 minutes depending upon size of shrimp). Serve at once. "Delicious with homemade mayonnaise."

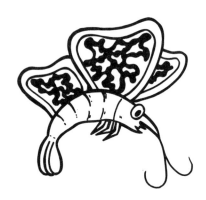

HOLDING PATTERN CASSEROLES AND STEWS

HOLDING and REHEATING FOOD

Unfortunately, many times delayed schedules are a pilot's fate. We all know that food which is held hot or reheated is not as tasty or nutritious as food served immediately after preparation. Refer to the holding and reheating food check list for procedures on reverse side.

HOLDING and REHEATING FOOD CHECK LIST

Casseroles:
From room temperature, place in 325 degree preheated oven.
Pancakes:
Place on kitchen cloth and wrap cloth between layers in 200 degree preheated oven.
Deep-fat Fried Foods:
Place in a pan over a rack, reheat uncovered in 250 degree preheated oven.
Vegetables:
Use a double boiler and reheat over hot water, do not cover.
Soups:
Reheat just to boiling point, serve at once.
Sauces:
Hold well in vacuum containers.
Creams and Egg Sauces:
Use a double boiler and reheat over hot water.
Pies and Cakes:
Place baking sheet under the pie or cake shiny side down to deflect heat and prevent further browning in a 250 degree oven.
Whole Roast:
From room temperature, reheat in oven at 200 degrees.
Creamed Dishes:
Place in a container of hot water covering about ⅔ of the container to be reheated. Place in 250 degree oven.

For short periods of time one may use: electric trays, infra-red lamps, chafing dish, steam tray, oven steam drawer, a warm sunny window or the top of the freezer. STANDARD CERTIFIED HOLDING TEMPERATURE IS 140 DEGREES FAHRENHEIT.

First Class Chili

1 large onion, chopped
1 green pepper, seeded and chopped
1 tablespoon vegetable oil
2 pounds lean ground beef, coarsely ground
2 dashes paprika
3 bay leaves
4 whole cloves
1 ounce semi-sweet chocolate, shaved
1 teaspoon salt
3 tablespoons chili powder
2 Tabasco shakes
¼ teaspoon black pepper
3 15-ounce cans red kidney beans, not drained
1 15-ounce can red kidney beans with chili gravy,
    not drained
1 8-ounce can tomato sauce
1 16-ounce can whole peeled tomatoes

In a large heavy pot saute onion and green pepper in oil; add beef
and brown. Add next 8 ingredients; stir and cook 2 minutes. Add
next 4 ingredients; stir to mix well. Cover and simmer for 2 hours.
Serve hot with certified rice. Serves: 15 - 20

YANKEE Pot Roast

2 beef bouillon cubes
½ cup water, cold
½ cup flour, all-purpose
1 teaspoon salt
¼ teaspoon black pepper
1 8-ounce can tomato sauce
4 pounds beef rump roast, boneless
3 medium carrots, peeled and sliced in 1 inch
    chunks
2 medium onions, quartered
8 new potatoes, whole
3 ribs celery, cut in 1 inch slices
1 medium red or green pepper, seeded and cut in 1
    inch strips

Dissolve bouillon cubes in water. In a large heavy pot combine bouillon, flour, salt, pepper and tomato sauce; stir to blend. Place roast in pot and vegetables along sides. Spoon sauce over roast and vegetables. Cover and bake at 325 for 2 hours or until tender. Serves: 6 - 8

Star Talk Seafood Pie

Shell:

> 10 ounces flour, all-purpose
> ⅛ teaspoon salt
> ½ teaspoon baking powder
> 5 ounces shortening
> 1 egg, beaten
> 1 ounce milk
> 4 ounces water

Combine dry ingredients and cut in shortening. Add liquids and mix briskly. Shape into a ball and roll out on a floured board or pastry cloth large enough to overlap a 9 inch pie pan. Fit dough to cover pan and sides.

Filling:

> 4 ounces smoked salmon
> 1 tablespoon corn starch
> 2 teaspoons water, cold
> 4 large eggs, beaten
> 10 ounces milk
> 1 tablespoon parsley, chopped
> 1 tablespoon chives, chopped
> 1 tablespoon onion, chopped
> 1 tablespoon butter
> 10 ounces crab meat
> 4 ounces Swiss cheese, grated
> salt and pepper to taste

Spread smoked salmon on bottom of shell. Mix corn starch with water to blend and stir in eggs, milk, parsley and chives. Pour over salmon in shell. Saute onion in the butter until tender and transparent. Spread over shell. Layer crab meat and cheese. Sprinkle salt and pepper to taste. Bake at 350 degrees for 35 minutes. Serves: 6

Chicken Casserole with Vegetables

4 chicken breasts, split
2 tablespoons flour
3 tablespoons cooking oil
1 onion, cut in 8 wedges
2 small zucchini, cut in half
1 yellow squash, chunky sliced
2 small potatoes, cut in half
1 4-ounce can button mushrooms, drained
3 fresh tomatoes, quartered
1 8-ounce can tomato sauce
1 teaspoon dried basil leaves
½ teaspoon garlic powder
½ teaspoon lemon pepper
½ teaspoon seasoned salt
¼ cup butter, melted

Wash and dry the chicken breasts and dust with flour. Heat oil in skillet and brown chicken on high heat. Place chicken in a casserole dish and add remaining ingredients. Cover and bake at 325 degrees for 1 hour. Serves: 4

Chicken to Fly

6 chicken pieces, skinned
2 tablespoons butter
1 large onion, quartered
2 carrots, peeled and sliced
2 ribs celery, sliced
1 10¾-ounce can cream of chicken soup
salt and black pepper to taste

Brown chicken in hot butter on both sides. Place in baking dish. Cover with onion, carrots, celery, soup and seasonings. Bake at 325 degrees for 1 hour covered. Serves: 6

Spring Lamb Stew

3 pounds lamb shoulder, cut into 1½ inch squares
salt and pepper to taste
4 tablespoons oil
2 small onions, chopped
1 clove garlic, chopped
2 tablespoons flour
1 glass chablis
3 cups chicken broth
2 tablespoons tomato paste
1 bay leaf
pinch of thyme
6 small peeled potatoes
1 teaspoon chopped parsley
1 pound fresh mixed vegetables

Brown meat on all sides with oil in skillet. Transfer the meat to casserole, season with salt and pepper, add onion and garlic. Simmer for two minutes. Stir in flour. Add wine, broth, tomato paste, bay leaf, thyme and parsley. Bring slowly to a boil, cover, reduce heat and simmer for 45 minutes. Add potatoes and mixed vegetables. Cover and cook for 15 minutes more or until vegetables are tender. Sprinkle more parsley over stew before serving. Serves: 6

LA BRASSERIE
202 South Main Street
Orange, California
(714) 639-7264

OSHKOSH Goulash

2 medium onions, chopped
1 green pepper, chopped
2 tablespoons butter
2 pounds rump roast, cubed
1 tablespoon paprika
1 teaspoon salt
water, warm
1 8-ounce can tomato sauce
2 dashes hot sauce
1 cup sour cream

In a large heavy skillet saute onions and green pepper in butter. Add cubed roast, paprika and salt; stir and saute. Add enough water to barely cover. Cover skillet and bake at 325 degrees for 3 hours. Remove and stir in tomato sauce, hot sauce and sour cream; heat thoroughly, but do not boil. Serve hot with noodles or spatzel. Serves: 8

No STALL Stew

2 garlic cloves, minced
1 potato, cubed
2 onions, chopped
2 tablespoons butter
2 pounds lean ground beef
1½ tablespoons salt
¼ teaspoon pepper
2½ tablespoons flour, all-purpose
1 16-ounce can stewed tomatoes
1 16-ounce package frozen mixed vegetables

Saute garlic, potatoes and onions in butter. Add beef, salt and pepper. Cook until beef is not red. Add flour; blend. Add tomatoes and vegetables; mix well. Cover and simmer for 45 minutes. Serves: 8

Layover Hamburger Casserole

2 onions, chopped
2 tablespoons butter
1 pound ground beef
1 green pepper, seeded and chopped
5 ribs celery, sliced
1 6-ounce package noodles
1 large can cream style corn
1 teaspoon salt
2 dashes black pepper
potato chips

Saute onions in butter until tender. Add beef and brown. Add green pepper and celery; cook 5 minutes. Prepare noodles according to package directions; drain. Add noodles, corn, salt and pepper to beef mixture; stir. Pour into 2 quart baking dish and cover with potato chips. Bake at 350 degrees for 30 minutes. Serves: 6

Light Chop with Potatoes

6 center-cut lean pork chops, thin
salt and pepper to taste
1 tablespoon vegetable oil
1 10¾-ounce can cream of mushroom soup
½ cup sour cream
¼ cup water
2 tablespoons parsley, chopped
1 medium onion, sliced thinly
½ teaspoon salt
2 cups baking potatoes, sliced thinly

Brown and season chops in oil turning once. In a mixing bowl blend soup, sour cream, water, parsley, onion and salt. Place 3 chops in a shallow baking dish, cover chops with soup mixture. Layer potatoes on soup mixture. Place 3 chops on top. Bake covered at 375 degrees for 1 hour. Serves: 6

North West Tuna Casserole

1 large onion, chopped
1 8-ounce can mushrooms, sliced and drained
¼ cup celery, sliced
3 tablespoons butter
1 6½-ounce can tuna, flaked
1 cup frozen peas
1 cup rice, raw uncooked
2 cups water
1 10¾-ounce can cream of celery soup
2 tablespoons soy sauce
8 black olives, sliced (optional)

Saute onions, mushrooms and celery in butter. Stir in tuna, peas, rice, water, soup and soy sauce. Pour into 3 quart casserole; place olives over top. Bake at 350 degrees for 1 hour. Serves: 6

"A favorite family recipe from my friend Marilyn Marx. Once upon a time, we were stewardesses."

Winning Weiner WINGERS

1 7-ounce package elbow macaroni
1 pound beef frankfurters, quartered
1 10¾-ounce can cream of celery soup
1 cup sour cream
1 medium carrot, peeled and shredded
1 small onion, chopped
¼ cup green pepper, chopped
½ teaspoon dill weed

Prepare macaroni according to package directions; drain. Combine all ingredients and mix well. Pour into a greased 2 quart baking dish. Bake covered at 350 degrees for 35 minutes. Serves: 6

BARNSTORMER Lamb Casserole

2 tablespoons butter
1 small onion, chopped
½ teaspoon ginger
1 10½-ounce can tomato soup
½ can water
1 teaspoon worcestershire sauce
1 bay leaf
¼ teaspoon all spice
2 tablespoons raw honey
1½ pounds lean lamb, cubed
½ cup flour, all-purpose
2 tablespoons vegetable oil
2 ounces raisins

Melt butter in a sauce pan; saute onion and ginger until golden. Add tomato soup, water, worcestershire sauce, bay leaf, all spice and honey. Cook on medium heat to a full boil; boil 1 minute. Remove from heat and pour liquid through a strainer; reserve liquid. Coat lamb with flour and saute in oil until golden. Combine lamb with liquid in a 4 quart casserole with cover; sprinkle raisins. Baked covered at 350 degrees for 1½ hours. Serves: 6

'You look a little shy; let me introduce you to that leg of mutton," said the Red Queen. 'Alice – Mutton; Mutton – Alice'

ALICE'S ADVENTURES IN WONDERLAND
Lewis Carroll

Tango Tangy Acapulco Enchiladas

2 cups cooked chicken, diced
⅓ cup green onion, minced
⅓ cup slivered almonds
½ teaspoon salt
3 cups enchilada sauce (mild)
8 tortillas
½ cup sour cream
1 4-ounce package cheddar cheese, shredded
¼ cup sliced ripe olives
chopped green chilies (optional)

Combine chicken, onions, almonds and salt. Heat sauce. Dip tortillas one at a time in the sauce. Remove and fill with chicken mixture. Top mixture with 1 tablespoon sour cream. Roll up and place in a baking casserole. Continue with each tortilla. Sprinkle with cheese and olives. Bake at 350 degrees for 15 minutes. Remove and drizzle with extra sauce. Yield: 8
Variation: Substitute lean ground beef for chicken.

The Wright Casserole

1 cup onion, chopped
2 tablespoons vegetable oil
1 pound lean ground beef
3 cups noodles, uncooked
3 cups tomato juice
2 teaspoons salt·
1 teaspoon celery salt
dash of black pepper
2 teaspoons worcestershire sauce
1 cup sour cream

Continued on next page →

The Wright Casserole (Continued)

Saute onion in oil until tender. Add beef and brown lightly; drain off excess liquid. Place noodles in layer over beef. Combine remaining ingredients except sour cream; pour over noodles to moisten. Bring to a boil, cover and simmer until noodles are tender (about 30 minutes). Stir in sour cream; heat thoroughly, but do not boil. Garnish with onion rings if desired. Serves: 4

"A favorite family recipe from Aunt Mary Jane."

STEADY GREEN Peppers

1 12-ounce package elbow macaroni
3 large green peppers, cut in half and seeded
1 pound lean ground beef
1 tablespoon vegetable oil
¼ teaspoon chili powder
½ teaspoon salt
¼ teaspoon black pepper
1 cup cheddar cheese, shredded
1 4-ounce jar pimento, chopped and drained
1 15-ounce can chili with beans
1 teaspoon oregano
Parmesan cheese

Prepare macaroni according to package directions; drain. Cook green peppers in boiling salted water 2 - 3 minutes; drain. In a sauce pan brown beef in oil; drain. Season beef with chili powder, salt and pepper. Add cheese, pimento, beans and oregano; mix well; simmer 3 minutes. Fold in macaroni. Spoon into green pepper halves and sprinkle cheese. May be frozen at this point or put under broiler 3 minutes to serve immediately. Serves: 6

Alternate: Forget the green peppers and prepare the remaining ingredients as a casserole.

Chicken A la Captain

1½ cups mushrooms, sliced
2 tablespoons butter
3 cups chicken, boiled and sliced
1 tablespoon green pepper, shredded
1½ cups chicken broth
4 egg yolks
¾ cup whipping cream
salt and black pepper to taste

In a large skillet saute mushrooms in butter. Add chicken, green pepper and broth; simmer on low heat covered 10 minutes. Beat the egg yolks and whipping cream until foamy; add 2 tablespoons hot broth mixture and stir into chicken mixture. Stir and heat well, but do not boil. Add seasoning. Serve over buttered toast or rice. Serves: 6

*"Keep a good table and look
after the ladies."*

Napoleon Bonaparte

Red Baron Beef

3 pounds lean stew beef, cubed
1 10¾-ounce can cream of mushroom soup
1 10½-ounce can onion soup
1 cup red wine
1 6-ounce can mushrooms, sliced and drained
2 ounces cognac

Combine all ingredients except cognac in a 3 quart baking casserole; stir to blend. Cover and cook 3½ hours at 350 degrees. Remove and stir in cognac. Cover and cook at 350 degrees 30 minutes longer. Serve hot with mashed potatoes. Serves: 8

THE COOKIE SUITCASE

*"Basic Standard
Certified Equipment"*

Pilots' Bow-Tie Cookies

½ stick butter, soft
1½ cups sugar
6 eggs, beaten
½ cup milk
½ teaspoon salt
2 teaspoons vegetable oil
1 teaspoon rum extract
1 tablespoon vanilla extract
2 teaspoons lemon extract
2 tablespoons anisette liqueur
3 pounds flour, all-purpose
cooking oil for deep frying
powdered sugar

Cream butter and sugar. Add eggs and blend. Add all the other ingredients except the flour; mix well. Add the flour gradually until the dough is like biscuit dough. Divide the dough into 3 parts, wrap with waxpaper and refrigerate 3 - 4 hours. Roll out dough on pastry cloth or floured board, using 1 part at a time. Roll dough paper-thin (⅛ inch). Cut the dough into strips; 6 inches long and ½ inch wide. Tie each strip into a bow-tie. Fry in deep hot oil (360 degrees) preheated. Fry until lightly browned (about 7 minutes). Drain and cool on paper towels. Dust with powdered sugar. Store in tight flight bag. Place in cookie suitcase, ready to travel. Yield: 5 dozen

Airplane Cut-Out Cookies

1 cup sugar
1 stick butter, soft
2 eggs
2½ cups flour, all-purpose
2 teaspoons baking powder
1 teaspoon vanilla extract
½ teaspoon almond extract

Cream sugar and butter, add eggs and beat well. Combine flour with baking powder and add to creamed mixture. Mix well and add flavorings. Form into a ball, wrap in waxpaper and chill 2 hours. Roll out on floured pastry board ⅛ inch thick. Cut into airplane shapes using cutter. Sprinkle with sugar sprinkles or hand-paint. Place on lightly greased baking sheet and bake at 375 degrees for 6 - 8 minutes. Yield: 4 dozen

Airplane Cookie Paint Category I:

¼ teaspoon water
1 egg yolk, beaten
food coloring

Mix water and egg yolk well. Divide mixture into 2 small cups and tint with desired coloring. Add a few drops of water if paint thickens. Prepare 1 recipe paint for each 2 colors desired. Apply paint with art brush to unbaked cookies.

Continued on next page →

Airplane Cut-Out Cookies (Continued)

Airplane Cookie Paint Category II:

> 1 box powdered sugar, sifted
> 2 egg whites, beaten stiff
> juice of 1 lemon or water
> food coloring

Gradually add sugar to egg white and add lemon juice. Cover with damp cloth until ready to use. Tint with food coloring. To make pure white add a very small amount of blue to prevent grey. After paint has been applied, sprinkles or other decoration may be applied if desired. Apply paint to baked and completely cooled airplane cookies.

Cook-While-You-Fly-Cookies

2 egg whites
¼ teaspoon cream of tartar
dash of salt
⅔ cup sugar
¼ teaspoon vanilla extract
1 cup pecans, chopped finely
1 cup semi-sweet chocolate morsels, optional

Preheat ovens to 350 degrees. Line 3 15½ x 12 inch baking sheets with foil and lightly butter. Using electric mixer, combine egg whites with cream of tartar and salt; beat until stiff. Gradually add the sugar. Beat well. Mix in vanilla and nuts. Semi-sweet chocolate morsels may be added at this time if desired. Drop 12 teaspoonfuls on each foil-lined baking sheet. Place in ovens and turn off. "Fly for 8 hours and return to find cookies baked and ready to eat." Yield: 3 dozen. (For electric ovens only)

Just Plane Good Sugar Cookies

1 cup butter, soft
1¼ cups sugar
2 eggs
1 teaspoon vanilla extract
2½ cups flour, all-purpose
1½ teaspoons baking powder
¼ teaspoon salt

Using an eletric mixer cream butter and sugar well. Add eggs and vanilla and blend well. Sift dry ingredients together and add gradually. Wrap dough in waxpaper and chill in refrigerator 2 hours. Roll out on a floured and sugared board to ¼ inch thickness. Cut out with airplane cookie cutter. Bake at 375 degrees for 8 - 10 minutes. Yield: 2 dozen

Gear Kiss Cookies

1 cup butter
½ cup sugar
1 teaspoon vanilla extract
½ teaspoon almond extract
1¾ cups flour, all-purpose
1 cup pecans, finely chopped
1 9-ounce package chocolate kiss candy
powdered sugar

Beat butter, sugar and vanilla until creamy. Stir in almond extract. Stir in flour and chopped nuts only to blend. Wrap in waxpaper and chill 30 minutes. Cover each chocolate kiss candy with a scant soup spoonful of the dough; cover each kiss completely. Place 2 inches apart onto ungreased baking sheet. Bake at 350 degrees for 10 - 12 minutes. Remove with a spatula and cool on waxpaper. Dust with powdered sugar. "Store in Cookie Suitcase." Yield: 2 dozen

"Stick to your sphere;
or, if you insist, as you
have the right,
On spreading your wings
for a loftier flight,
The moral is – Take care
where you light."

J. T. Trowbridge

Scattered to Broken Lace Cookies

1 cup old-fashioned oats
½ tablespoon flour, all-purpose
1 cup sugar
¼ teaspoon salt
1 stick butter, melted and hot
1 egg, beaten
½ teaspoon vanilla extract

Mix all dry ingredients well. Stir in hot butter, egg and vanilla. Cover a baking sheet with foil and lightly butter. Drop cookie mixture with a teaspoon onto baking sheet 2 inches apart. Bake at 350 degrees 7 - 10 minutes (until golden brown). Cool 3 - 5 minutes and peel off foil. Yield: 1 dozen

Savory Flight Cookies

2 cups flour, all-purpose
2 sticks butter, melted
¼ cup granulated sugar
2 cups pecans, chopped finely
powdered sugar

Combine first 4 ingredients. Mix and form into small balls. Bake on ungreased baking sheet at 300 degrees for 45 minutes. Remove with spatula and roll in powdered sugar while hot. Cool and reroll in powdered sugar. "Store in tightly covered flight bag." Yield: 3 dozen

Apple Squares
"Under a Coconut HOOD"

2 cups sugar
1½ cups vegetable oil
3 eggs
2 teaspoons vanilla extract
3 cups flour, all-purpose
1 teaspoon baking soda
¼ teaspoon salt
3 cups apples, peeled and sliced thinly
1 cup walnuts, chopped coarsely

Using an electric mixer beat sugar, oil, eggs and vanilla well. Add flour, soda and salt. Mix well. Fold in apples and nuts. Pour into buttered baking pan (13 x 10 inch). Bake at 350 degrees for 35 minutes.

Note: Winesap is a good tangy apple for this dessert.

Coconut Hood:

1 stick butter
1 cup light brown sugar
¼ cup evaporated milk
1 teaspoon lemon extract
1 3½-ounce can coconut, flaked

Heat butter, sugar, milk and flavoring on medium heat and cook for about 3 minutes. Pour over cooled apple cake. Top with coconut. Cut into squares. Yield: 24 squares

"A family favorite from Aunt Christine."

HAVE Chocolate Chip Cookies WILL TRAVEL

2 sticks butter, melted
2 eggs
½ cup light brown sugar
1 cup granulated sugar
2 teaspoons vanilla extract
2 cups flour, all-purpose
1 teaspoon salt
1 teaspoon baking soda
1 cup pecans, chopped
1 12-ounce package chocolate chips

Using an electric mixer beat butter, eggs, sugars and vanilla until light and fluffy. Gently add dry ingredients, blend well. Stir in nuts and chips. Drop from a soup spoon onto ungreased baking sheet, 2 inches apart. Bake at 375 degrees for 8 - 10 minutes. Remove with a spatula while hot and cool on waxpaper.
Yield: 3 dozen

Boarding Tutti-Frutti Surprises

2 eggs
1 cup powdered sugar
3 tablespoons butter, melted
¾ cup flour, all-purpose
1½ teaspoons baking powder
1 teaspoon salt
1 cup pecans, chopped finely
¾ cup candied fruit, chopped

Beat eggs until foamy and then beat in sugar. Add butter and beat well. Sift dry ingredients together and add a little at a time to the batter. Fold in nuts and fruit. Pour into buttered 8 x 8 inch square baking pan. Bake at 325 degrees for 30 - 35 minutes. Yield: 16

Airmail Oatmeal Cookies

¾ cup solid shortening
1 cup light brown sugar
½ cup granulated sugar
1 egg
¼ cup water
1 teaspoon vanilla extract
1 cup flour, all-purpose
1 teaspoon salt
1 teaspoon cinnamon
½ teaspoon cloves
½ teaspoon baking soda
1 cup raisins
1 cup pecans, chopped
3 cups quick-cooking oats

Use an electric mixer to mix first 6 ingredients. Blend well. Remove from mixer and stir in remaining ingredients. Drop with a soup spoon onto an ungreased baking sheet; placing 1 inch apart. Bake at 350 degrees for 12 - 15 minutes. Yield: 3 dozen

Fly-In Persimmon Cookies

1 cup sugar
½ cup solid shortening
1 egg
1 teaspoon soda
1 cup persimmon pulp
2 cups flour, all-purpose
1 teaspoon baking powder
½ teaspoon salt
¼ teaspoon cinnamon
¼ teaspoon nutmeg
¼ teaspoon cloves
1 cup chopped dates or coconut
1 cup pecans, chopped

Beat sugar, shortening and egg well. In a small bowl add soda to persimmon pulp and mix well; combine with sugar mixture. Sift dry ingredients together and add to batter; mix thoroughly. Fold in dates or coconut and pecans. Drop onto ungreased baking sheet. Place 2 inches apart. Bake at 350 degrees for 10 - 15 minutes. Remove with spatula and cool on waxpaper. Yield: 2 dozen. "These are delicious, soft and moist cookies."

Note: Persimmons are available at the market in August and September. To obtain pulp: clean and wash persimmons and press through a colander to remove seeds. The pulp freezes well and lasts for many months.

Lazy Eight Cakey Brownies

1 cup sugar
4 tablespoons cocoa
1 stick butter, melted
2 eggs, beaten
1 cup flour, all-purpose
½ teaspoon baking powder
⅛ teaspoon salt
½ teaspoon vanilla extract
1 cup pecans, chopped

Mix sugar and cocoa and blend in butter. Add eggs and mix well.
Combine flour, baking powder and salt; add to batter. Stir in
vanilla and nuts. Pour batter into a buttered 8 x 8 inch baking pan.
Bake at 350 degrees for 25 minutes. Cool before cutting.
Yield: 16

*"Measure a thousand times
and cut once."*

Turkish proverb

Layover Pecan Squares

4 eggs, beaten
1 box light brown sugar
1 tablespoon evaporated milk
2 cups biscuit mix
2 cups pecans, chopped
1 teaspoon vanilla extract
powdered sugar

Combine eggs and brown sugar in saucepan. Cook on medium heat for 15 minutes; stir. Add milk, biscuit mix, nuts and vanilla. Stir to blend well. Pour into buttered 10 x 10 x 2 inch baking pan. Bake at 350 degrees for 25 - 30 minutes. Cut while hot and roll in powdered sugar. Yield: 25

Pecan Tea Cakes

Shell:

1 stick butter, soft
1 3-ounce cream cheese, soft
1 cup flour, all-purpose

Combine all ingredients; blend well. Chill 1 hour. Roll on pastry cloth into 24 balls. Press each ball into a well greased teacake size muffin tin to form shell. Set aside.

Filling:

1 egg, beaten
¾ cup light brown sugar
1 tablespoon butter, melted
⅔ cup chopped pecans
1 teaspoon vanilla extract

Combine egg, sugar and butter. Mix well. Add pecans and vanilla. Place 1 tablespoon of filling in each shell. Bake at 325 degrees for 15 - 20 minutes. Cool before serving. Yield: 24

Aurora Borealis Delights

1 cup sugar
1 cup brown sugar
1 cup butter, soft
2 eggs
2 cups flour, all-purpose
½ teaspoon baking soda
2 teaspoons baking powder
½ teaspoon salt
1½ cups old-fashioned oats
1 cup coconut
1 cup dates, chopped
1 cup raisins
1 cup pecans, chopped
1 teaspoon lemon rind, grated
1 teaspoon orange rind, grated
½ teaspoon orange extract
½ teaspoon vanilla extract
candied cherries, halved

Combine sugars and butter in electric mixer and mix at medium speed. Add eggs and beat well. Combine dry ingredients and fruits; add to batter; mix well. Stir in nuts, rinds and extracts. Drop by teaspoonfuls onto greased cookie sheet two inches apart. Press a cherry half into each cookie. Bake at 350 degrees for 15 minutes. Cool on cookie sheet a few minutes then on waxpaper or cooling racks. Yield: 4 dozen

Aurora Borealis

The heavens were at play tonight
And I perchance could watch;
The Northern Lights danced merrily
And a star got so excited it dropped

COME FLY WITH ME

Patricia Moran

Date Nut Roll Over

1 cup dates, chopped
¾ cup walnuts, chopped coarsely
3 tablespoons butter
1½ teaspoons soda
1 cup water, boiling hot
2 eggs
1 cup sugar
1½ cups flour, all-purpose
½ teaspoon vanilla extract

Place dates, nuts, butter and soda in mixing bowl; add boiling water; set aside. Beat eggs and sugar until light and fluffy. Add the flour; mix thoroughly. Add the date mixture to batter and mix with the vanilla. Pour ¾ full into buttered and flour-dusted baking powder cans (5¼ inch) or small round tins. Bake at 325 degrees for 35 - 40 minutes. Remove from containers while hot; carefully. Cool on racks. Wrap in foil or plastic. To serve: cut into slices and spread with cream cheese if desired. Yield: 3 rolls

Let's Get Rolling Pecan Logs

2 cups marshmallow cream
3½ cups powdered sugar, sifted
¼ teaspoon butter, soft
1 teaspoon vanilla extract
2 tablespoons heavy cream
1 14-ounce package caramels
1 cup pecans, chopped finely

Combine marshmallow cream, sugar, butter and vanilla. Knead and form into 3 logs or rolls. Wrap in waxpaper and freeze. In saucepan with cover combine cream and caramels. Melt covered on low heat. Roll frozen logs in melted caramels; then roll in chopped pecans. Cut in slices to serve. Yield: 3 logs

TOP GUM Fudgy Brownies

2 sticks butter
4 squares chocolate, unsweetened
4 eggs
2 cups sugar
1 teaspoon vanilla extract
1 cup flour, all-purpose
¼ teaspoon salt
2 cups pecans, chopped coarsely

Melt butter and chocolate in saucepan over low heat; stirring to blend butter and chocolate; set aside. Using an electric mixer, beat eggs well and gradually add 1 cup sugar. Beat well on high speed. Gradually add second cup of sugar and beat until thick and fluffy. Remove batter from mixer and stir in vanilla and chocolate mixture. Fold in flour, salt and nuts until just blended. Pour equally into 2 buttered 8 x 8 inch square baking pans. Bake at 350 degrees for 25 minutes. Cool before cutting. Yield: 32 servings

"Foil pans are good travelers."

Sunset Lemon Glares

2 cups flour, all-purpose
2 sticks butter, melted
½ cup powdered sugar
4 eggs, beaten
2 cups granulated sugar
juice of 3 lemons
¼ cup flour, all-purpose
1 teaspoon baking powder
additional powdered sugar

Combine and mix flour, butter and powdered sugar. Press into a buttered 10 x 14 inch baking pan. Bake at 325 degrees for 15 minutes. Combine eggs, granulated sugar, lemon juice, flour and baking powder. Stir only to mix. Pour on top of hot crust. Bake at 350 degrees for 25 minutes. Cool. Dust with additional powdered sugar and cut. Yield: 32

Meringue Stars

2 eggs whites, room temperature
¼ teaspoon cream of tartar
½ cup sugar
½ teaspoon vanilla extract

Combine egg whites and cream of tartar using electric mixer. Beat on high speed until eggs form peaks. Gradually add the sugar until eggs form stiff peaks. Beat in vanilla. Place mixture in a decorating bag fitted with star tip ½ inch size. Squeeze gently to form star shape onto foil lined baking sheet. Place stars 1 inch apart. Decorate stars with sugars, nuts or candies if desired. Bake at 300 degrees for 15 minutes. Turn off oven and let stars rest 30 minutes with oven door closed. Yield: 1 dozen

Note: For electric oven only.

Over the Fence Date Bars

2 8-ounce boxes pitted dates, chopped
1 cup granulated sugar
1 cup water, warm
½ cup shortening
1 cup brown sugar
1½ cups flour, all-purpose
1 teaspoon soda
½ teaspoon salt
1¾ cups old-fashioned oats

Combine dates, granulated sugar and water in saucepan. Cook on medium heat until like jam. Set aside. Cream shortening and brown sugar; add dry ingredients and oats. This will be crumbly. Mix well. Use waxpaper to line a 9 x 13 inch baking pan. Spread and press firmly one-half of the oat mixture. Spread all the date mixture over the oat layer. Finish the top with the remaining oat mixture. Spread and press firmly. Bake at 350 degrees for 30 minutes. Cool before cutting. Yield: 12 bars

Adventure Chocolate Fudge Bars

Bottom Crust Layer:

½ cup almonds, ground finely in processor
1 cup flour, all-purpose
¼ cup sugar
½ teaspoon salt
1 stick butter, melted
1 egg, beaten

Combine the almonds, flour, sugar, salt and butter. Mix until it resembles coarse meal. Add the egg and blend. Press into a 8 x 8 x 2 inch baking pan and bake at 350 degrees for 18 - 20 minutes.

Top Fudge Layer:

1 can sweetened condensed milk
2 tablespoons sugar
3 tablespoons butter
¼ teaspoon almond extract
1 ounce unsweetened chocolate
¼ cup almonds, sliced

Combine the milk, sugar, butter and extract in a heavy saucepan; heat on low heat until hot and sugar dissolved. Remove from heat and add the chocolate. Stir to melt and blend the chocolate. Spread the fudge over warm bottom crust evenly. Sprinkle the sliced almonds. Cool and cut into bars. Yield: 12

Over the Top
Nectarine Cheesecake Bars

Bottom Cake Layer:

½ cup sugar
¼ teaspoon salt
½ teaspoon baking powder
½ cup flour, all-purpose
½ stick butter, melted
1 egg, beaten

Combine the sugar, salt, baking powder and flour. Mix well and add the butter, blending until it resembles small peas. Add the egg and mix well. Press evenly into a buttered 8 x 8 x 2 inch baking pan. Set aside.

Top Cheese layer:

1 8-ounce cream cheese, soft
4 tablespoons sugar
1 teaspoon vanilla extract
1 egg
1 tablespoon flour, all-purpose
1 teaspoon fresh lemon juice
⅛ teaspoon salt
1 fresh nectarine, sliced thinly

In blender or electric mixer combine the cheese, 2 tablespoons sugar and vanilla. Blend well. Add the egg, flour, lemon juice and salt. Blend until smooth. Spread evenly over the bottom cake layer. Arrange the nectarine slices over the top and sprinkle with 2 tablespoons sugar. Bake at 350 degrees for 20 minutes. Cool and cut into bars. Keep chilled. Yield: 12 bars.(Peaches may be substituted for nectarines)

– Notes –

CANDY

"How sweet it is"
Jackie Gleason

"Do you find yourself "lost" in the galley?"

PANIC PROCEDURE!

**Contact your nearest FSS
(Food Service Station)**

Request a DFS (Directions for Scoot)

Rainbow Mints

3 cups sugar
1 cup water, boiling
1 tablespoon butter
2 teaspoons peppermint extract
food coloring

In a small heavy saucepan add sugar and water; stir to dissolve. Cook on medium heat covered until boiling. Remove cover and hold butter in the steam to gradually let it melt off the spoon. Continue to boil to hard boil stage (do not stir) (254 F degrees). Add extract. Pour onto buttered marble slab. Cool. Separate a portion for each color desired. Add coloring (about 2 drops for each color desired. Pull until creamy and cut into pieces with scissors. Yield: 1 pound

Touch N' Go Kisses

½ teaspoon vanilla extract
¾ cup light brown sugar
1 egg white, beaten stiff
2 cups pecan halves

Gradually add vanilla and brown sugar to egg white. Stir in pecans. Spoon onto greased baking sheet. Bake at 350 degrees for 30 minutes. Turn off oven and wait 30 minutes before removing with a spatula. Yield: 24

Chocolate Drops At Altitude

1 14-ounce can condensed milk
2½ cups semisweet chocolate morsels
1 teaspoon vanilla extract
1 cup pecans, chopped

Combine condensed milk and chocolate morsels in a heavy
saucepan and cook over low heat until smooth. Remove from
heat and stir in vanilla and nuts. Place on wax paper in
teaspoonfuls. Let stand until firm. Yield: 2 pounds

Pralines

¾ cup light brown sugar
¾ cup granulated sugar
½ cup evaporated milk
1 tablespoon butter
1 teaspoon vanilla extract
1 cup pecan halves

Mix sugars and milk in a heavy saucepan. Cook on medium-low
heat to soft ball stage. Add butter and vanilla. Remove from heat
and beat 2 minutes until creamy and thick. Place quickly by
teaspoonfuls onto newspaper covered with waxpaper. Press a
pecan half every 5th praline before it sets. Yield: 18 - 24 pralines
the size of a 50¢ piece.

OVER GROSS CAKES and FROSTINGS

SAUCES and GLAZES

Black Forest Cake
(Schwarzwalder Kirschtorte)

1 9-inch chocolate sponge cake
1 can pitted dark sweet cherries
3 pints whipping cream
1 teaspoon vanilla extract
1½ cups sugar
3 ounces Kirschwasser (Cherry Brandy)
1 big bar semi-sweet chocolate
12 maraschino cherries

Slice sponge cake in three equally thick slices. Drain can of cherries well. Add ½ cup of sugar to juice and bring to a boil. Simmer for 5 minutes until thick like syrup. Let cool.
Add vanilla extract and one cup of sugar to heavy cream and whip until stiff. Sprinkle first layer of cake with syrup and 1 ounce of Kirschwasser. Put all drained cherries on same layer. Cover cherries generously with whipped cream.
Add next layer of cake. Sprinkle with syrup and Kirschwasser, add whipping cream. Repeat with third layer. Cover whole cake with rest of whipping cream and decorate with chocolate shavings. Garnish with maraschino cherries. Ready to serve.

Note: Pillsbury German Chocolate cake mix may be used for sponge cake.

Creative European Cuisine

WILLY COLN'S CHALET

WILLY COLN'S CHALET
2505 Whitney Avenue
Gretna, Louisiana 70053
(504) 361-3860

WILLY COLN'S
KALEIDOSCOPE
Canal Place – Third Level
New Orleans, Louisiana

Tunnel of Love Fudge Cake

1½ cups butter (3 sticks), soft
6 eggs
1½ cups sugar
2 cups flour, all-purpose
1 13.7-ounce package chocolate frosting mix, dry
2 cups walnuts, chopped coarsely

Beat butter at high speed until fluffy. Add the eggs one at a time; beating after each addition. Gradually add the sugar; beat until fluffy. By hand stir in the flour, dry frosting mix and walnuts until blended. Place evenly in a greased and floured bundt pan. Bake at 350 degrees for 50 minutes. Cool 2 hours before removing from pan. Serves: 8 - 10

"Disgustingly wonderful! It really does have a tunnel of fudge in the middle of each slice."

Mary Rose Dill

Four Day Shuttle Cake

1 package butter flavored cake mix
2 cups sugar
1 16-ounce carton sour cream
1 12-ounce package frozen coconut

Prepare cake mix as directed on package. Bake in 2 layers. Cool. Cut each layer in half. Combine sugar, sour cream and coconut; mix by hand. Chill 2 hours. Reserve 1 cup for cake top and spread remaining mixture between layers. Place cake in a covered cake container and refrigerate for 4 days. "A delicious coming home treat." Keep refrigerated.

INVERTED Pineapple Cake

Bottom mixture:

4 tablespoons butter
1 cup light brown sugar
5 maraschino cherries, cut in half
2 15-ounce cans crushed pineapple, drained

Melt butter in an 8 x 10 x 2 inch baking pan. Sprinkle brown sugar evenly. Place cherries round side down in a decorative pattern or at random. Spread pineapple carefully over all evenly. Set aside.

Batter:

¼ cup butter, soft
¾ cup sugar
1 egg
1 teaspoon vanilla extract
1½ cups cake flour
¼ teaspoon salt
2 teaspoons baking powder
½ cup milk

Cream butter, sugar, egg and extract. Sift dry ingredients and add alternately with the milk. Mix well. Pour over pineapple and bake at 350 degrees for 45 minutes. Cool slightly and invert.

Chocolate Pound Cake

2 sticks butter, soft
3 cups sugar
⅛ teaspoon salt
½ cup vegetable shortening
5 eggs
3 cups cake flour
1 cup milk
½ teaspoon baking powder
4 tablespoons cocoa

Cream butter, sugar, salt and vegetable shortening. Add eggs one at a time; beating after each addition. Add flour and milk alternately having added baking powder to the last part of the flour. Mix in cocoa well. Pour into greased and floured bundt pan or 10 inch tube pan. Place in a cold oven and bake at 300 degrees for 2 hours. Do not open oven until baking time is completed. Cool slightly before removing from pan. "Delicious served plain, glazed or with chocolate sauce."
Alternate: Omit the cocoa and add 1 teaspoon vanilla extract or lemon extract for basic pound cake.

Glaze:

1 cup powdered sugar, sifted
1 teaspoon vanilla extract
4 teaspoons milk, hot

Combine and mix ingredients until smooth. Drizzle warm glaze over warm cake. Allow to set before slicing.

Continued on next page →

Chocolate Pound Cake (Continued)

Chocolate Sauce:

3 egg yolks, beaten
1 cup sugar
1 cup evaporated milk
¼ cup butter
1 cup pecans, chopped finely
1 teaspoon vanilla extract

Combine egg yolks, sugar, milk and butter in a double boiler; cook on medium heat until thick. Stir in nuts and extract. Serve warm with pound cake. Keeps well in refrigerator and rewarms easily in double boiler or microwave. Yield: 3 cups

Taste 'N Go Prune Cake

2 cups sugar
1 cup vegetable oil
3 eggs
1 cup buttermilk
1 cup cooked prunes, chopped coarsely
2 cups flour, all-purpose
1 teaspoon baking soda
1 teaspoon salt
1 teaspoon cinnamon
1 teaspoon cloves
1 teaspoon nutmeg
1 teaspoon vanilla extract
1 cup pecans, chopped coarsely

Cream sugar, oil and eggs until fluffy. Blend in buttermilk and prunes. Sift all dry ingredients together and add to batter gradually. Stir in vanilla and pecans. Pour into a greased and floured bundt pan. Bake at 325 degrees for 1 hour.

High and Mighty Coconut Cake

3½ cups cake flour, sifted and measured
4 teaspoons baking powder
½ teaspoon salt
2 cups sugar
1 cup butter, soft
1 cup milk
1 teaspoon almond extract
¼ teaspoon vanilla extract
8 egg whites, beaten
coconut, flaked

Sift together flour, baking powder and salt. Cream sugar and
butter; add dry ingredients alternately with the milk. Add
extracts. Fold in egg whites. Pour into 3 (8 inch) waxpaper lined
cake pans. Bake at 375 degrees for 25 minutes. Cool layers on
racks completely before adding filling and frosting. After frosting
sprinkle cake completely with coconut. Serves: 18
"A wonderful cake for a celebration of wings party."

Filling:

1 cup sugar
3 tablespoons corn starch
pinch of salt
1 cup milk
2 cups coconut, flaked
2 tablespoons butter
1 teaspoon almond extract

Combine sugar with corn starch in a saucepan. Add salt and milk;
cook on low heat to dissolve. Stir and cook slowly to thicken. Stir
in coconut; cook until thickened. Add butter and extract. Cool.
Spread evenly between cooled cake layers.

Continued on next page →

High and Mighty Coconut Cake (Continued)

Frosting:

> 2 egg whites, unbeaten
> 1½ cups sugar
> ¼ teaspoon cream of tartar
> ⅓ cup water, cold
> dash salt
> 1 teaspoon vanilla extract

Combine egg whites, sugar, cream of tartar, water and salt in a double boiler. Cook on medium heat Beat with hand held electric beater for 1 minute. Continue cooking for 7 minutes beating constantly until mixture forms stiff peaks. Remove from heat and beat in extract. Spread onto cake immediately.

Certified Rich Pound Cake

> ½ pound butter, soft
> 3 cups sugar
> 6 eggs
> 3 cups cake flour
> ½ pint whipping cream
> 2 teaspoons vanilla extract

Cream butter with sugar until light and fluffy. Add eggs one at a time; beating after each addition. Add flour and cream alternately. Stir in extract. Pour into a greased and floured 10 inch tube pan. Place in a cold oven and bake at 325 degrees for 1½ hours. Cool before removing from pan.

"Fabulous" Mary Rose Dill

Far Horizon Orange Chiffon Cake

2 cups flour, all-purpose
1½ cups sugar
½ teaspoon salt
1 tablespoon baking powder
5 egg yolks
½ cup vegetable oil
1 teaspoon vanilla extract
¾ cup fresh orange juice
2 tablespoons orange rind, grated
8 egg whites
½ teaspoon cream of tartar

Combine flour, sugar, salt and baking powder in mixing bowl. Add egg yolks, vegetable oil, extract, orange juice and rind; blend and beat until smooth. Beat egg whites and cream of tartar until stiff. Fold into batter. Pour into a greased and floured 10 inch tube pan and bake at 325 degrees for 1 hour. Cool completely before adding glaze.

Glaze:

3 cups powdered sugar
¼ cup fresh orange juice
2 tablespoons orange rind, grated
2 tablespoons butter, melted

Combine sugar with orange juice and add remaining ingredients. Blend well. Drizzle glaze over cold cake.

Carrot Cake

2 cups sugar
1½ cups vegetable oil
4 eggs
2 cups flour, all-purpose
2 teaspoons baking powder
2 teaspoons baking soda
1 teaspoon salt
2 teaspoons cinnamon
3 cups carrots, peeled and grated coarsely
1 cup pecans, chopped coarsely

Cream sugar and oil. Add one egg at a time; beating well after each addition. Sift flour and all dry ingredients. Gradually add to batter. Stir in carrots and nuts; mix well. Pour batter equally among 3 cake pans, lined with waxpaper. Bake at 350 degrees for 25 - 30 minutes. Remove and cool on racks before frosting. Serves: 15

Frosting:

1 box powdered sugar
1 8-ounce cream cheese, soft
1 stick butter, soft
1 teaspoon vanilla extract
yellow food coloring

Combine sugar, cream cheese and butter at low speed to blend. Mix in extract and food coloring to desired color. Spread between cooled cake layers and cover cake completely.

Southern Fig Cake

2 cups flour, all-purpose
1 teaspoon salt
1 teaspoon cloves
1 teaspoon cinnamon
1 teaspoon nutmeg
1 teaspoon baking soda
1½ cups sugar
1 cup vegetable oil
3 eggs
1 cup buttermilk
1 cup fig preserves
1 teaspoon vanilla extract
1 cup pecans, chopped finely

Combine and mix all dry ingredients well. Blend in the vegetable oil. Add eggs one at a time; beating after each addition. Add buttermilk with the preserves. Mix well. Stir in extract and nuts. Pour into a greased and floured bundt pan. Bake at 350 degrees for 1 hour. Remove from the oven and immediately pour hot glaze over the cake while remaining in bundt pan. Cool before removing from pan. Serves: 8 - 10

Glaze:

½ stick butter
1 cup sugar
½ cup buttermilk
1 tablespoon white karo syrup
1 teaspoon vanilla extract

Place all ingredients in a small saucepan and bring to a boil; boil 3 minutes. Pour hot glaze over hot cake.

Coconut Pound Cake

6 eggs, separated
1 cup vegetable shortening
½ cup butter
1½ cups sugar
½ teaspoon almond extract
½ teaspoon coconut extract
1½ teaspoons baking powder
3 cups cake flour, sifted and measured
1 cup milk
2 cups coconut, flaked
powdered sugar

Cream egg yolks, shortening and butter until fluffy. Add sugar; beat well. Mix in extracts. Sift the baking powder with the flour. Gradually add flour alternately with the milk. Beat in coconut. Whip egg whites into stiff peaks; fold into batter. Pour into greased and floured bundt pan. Bake at 300 degrees for 2 hours. Cool and dust with powdered sugar or remove while warm and pour over warm glaze.

Glaze:

1 cup sugar
½ cup water
1 teaspoon almond extract

Combine ingredients in a small saucepan and bring to a boil for 2 minutes. Cool slightly. Pour warm glaze over warm cake.

King Cake

½ cup water
½ cup milk
4 tablespoons butter (½ stick)
3½ cups flour, all-purpose
¼ cup sugar
1 teaspoon salt
1 package active dry yeast
1 egg
vegetable oil

Combine water, milk and butter in small saucepan and heat on low heat until butter is melted. Set aside to reduce temperature to warm. Using an electic mixer, combine 1 cup flour, sugar, salt and yeast while gradually adding the warm milk mixture. Beat 2 minutes at medium speed. Add egg and 1 more cup flour and beat 2 minutes at high speed. Remove from mixer and gradually add the remaining 1½ cups flour to make a stiff dough. Knead dough 3 - 5 minutes on floured board until dough is smooth and not sticky. Grease top and bottom of dough lightly with vegetable oil. Cover with a kitchen cloth and place in a warm place free of drafts. Dough should double in bulk (about 2 hours). Prepare filling.

Filling:

2 cups brown sugar
2 teaspoons cinnamon
1 stick butter, melted

Combine brown sugar and cinnamon to make a sprinkle mixture. Melt butter. Set aside.

Punch down dough and knead 3 - 4 times. Divide into 2 parts. Roll one part into a 25 x 15 inch oblong. Spread with ¼ cup

Continued on next page →

King Cake (Continued)

melted butter. Sprinkle 1 cup of the brown sugar mixture over the butter. Begin with the wide side of the dough and roll lightly. Repeat procedure with the second part. Twist the 2 rolls and pinch and attach the ends together to form a ring. Place ring on a greased baking sheet (14 x 17 inch). Cover the ring with greased wax paper and a kitchen cloth. Place in a warm place until doubled in bulk (about 1½ hours). Bake at 375 degrees for 20 - 25 minutes. Cool. Spread icing on top and decorate with gold, purple and green sugars.

Icing:

> 1 cup powdered sugar, sifted
> 2 tablespoons milk, warm
> 1 teaspoon vanilla extract
> 1 teaspoon corn oil

Combine sugar, milk and vanilla and beat well. Add oil and beat until smooth and creamy. Additional milk may be added to correct consistency if the icing is too thick. Additional powdered sugar may be added to correct consistency if the icing is too thin. Icing should be a spreading consistency. Apply to cool cake. Add decorative sugars.

Decorative Sugars:

> ¾ cup sugar
> 1 teaspoon cinnamon
> yellow, green, blue and red food colors

Combine sugar and cinnamon and divide among three small bowls ¼ cup each. Using a small spoon combine sugar with yellow food coloring to make a desired gold color. Combine sugar with green food coloring to make a desired green color. Combine sugar with blue and some red to make a desired purple. Mix each color separately and well. Sprinkle the gold color on one of the

Continued on next page →

King Cake (Continued)

King Cake swells, sprinkle the next swell with green and the third one, sprinkle purple. Continue around the ring. Serves: 12

"Traditionally, a tiny toy baby is placed in the dough before the final rising and baked in the ring. This cake is great for a Mardi Gras Hangar Party. The recipe doubles easily, if you don't mind using your wing for rolling space."

Fly In Travel Cake

2 cups sugar
2 eggs
⅓ cup vegetable oil
1 15-ounce can crushed pineapple
2 cups flour, all-purpose
1½ teaspoons baking soda
1 pinch salt

Combine ingredients in order listed and mix well. Pour into a greased and floured 9 x 13 inch baking pan. Bake at 350 degrees for 40 minutes. Pour hot topping evenly over hot cake. Cool before slicing. Serves: 12 - 15

Topping:

1 cup sugar
1 stick butter
1 small can evaporated milk
1 teaspoon vanilla extract
1 cup pecans, chopped coarsely
1 cup coconut, flaked

Combine sugar, butter and milk in a small saucepan. Cook on medium heat; stir to blend. Bring to a boil for 5 minutes. Remove from heat; stir in extract, pecans and coconut. Pour hot topping over hot cake.

Apple Sky Cake

1¼ cups vegetable oil
2 cups sugar
3 large eggs
3 cups flour, all-purpose
1 teaspoon salt
1 teaspoon baking soda
1 teaspoon cinnamon
3 cups Winesap apples, peeled, cored and sliced
    thickly
1½ cups walnuts or pecans, chopped coarsely
1 teaspoon vanilla extract

Using an electric mixer, beat oil and sugar until opaque. Add eggs, one at a time, beating well after each addition. Sift flour, salt, soda and cinnamon together. Mix well with egg batter; remove from mixer. Stir in apples, nuts and vanilla (batter will be stiff). Spoon evenly into a greased and flour dusted bundt baking pan. Bake at 325 degrees for 1 hour and 15 minutes. Let cake rest for 10 minutes, then unmold and pour warm glaze over warm cake. Yield: 10 servings "Peaches may be substituted."

Glaze:

1 stick butter
1 cup light brown sugar
¼ cup cream
1 teaspoon vanilla extract

Melt butter in a small saucepan and stir in sugar. Add remaining ingredients, stir and bring to a boil. Boil 2½ minutes. Remove from heat and cool slightly. Pour over warm cake. Yield: 1½ cups

– Notes –

PIES and
PUDDINGS

"Cottleston, Cottleston, Cottleston Pie.
A fly can't bird, but a bird can fly.
Ask me a riddle and I reply:
Cottleston, Cottleston, Cottleston Pie."

POOH
Lewis Carroll

Black Bottom Pie

1½ cups crushed Zwieback
¼ cup powdered sugar
6 tablespoons melted butter
1 teaspoon cinnamon

Mix these ingredients well and place in pie pan and pat along the sides and bottom to make crust. Bake in moderate oven for 15 minutes. (Ginger crumbs can be used in place of zwieback)

1 tablespoon gelatin
2 cups rich milk
4 egg yolks, beaten lightly
1 cup sugar
4 teaspoons cornstarch
½ teaspoon vanilla
1½ squares melted unsweetened chocolate

Soak gelatin in ½ cup cold water. Scald milk. Combine egg yolks, sugar and cornstarch, stir in gradually milk and cook over hot water until custard will coat a spoon. Take out 1 cup of custard and add chocolate to it. Beat until well blended and cool. Add vanilla and pour into pie shell. Dissolve gelatin in remaining custard, cool, but do not permit to stiffen, stir in 1 teaspoon almond flavoring, 3 egg whites, ¼ teaspoon salt, ¼ cup sugar, ¼ teaspoon cream of tartar.
Beat egg whites and salt until blended, add cream of tartar and beat until stiff, gradually add sugar, fold in remaining custard and cover chocolate custard with almond flavored custard. Chill and set. Whip cup of heavy cream. Add 2 tablespoons of powdered sugar and spread over pie. ENJOY.

High Hampton Inn & Country Club

Cashiers, North Carolina 28717   William D. McKee, Jr.
Telephone 704-743-2411   Manager

Picnic Coconut Pie

1¼ cups coconut, flaked
½ cup heavy cream
¼ cup butter
1 cup sugar
3 eggs
1 teaspoon vanilla extract
1 9-inch pie shell, unbaked

Place coconut in a small bowl. Pour over the cream; set aside.
Cream butter and sugar; add eggs one at a time; beating well after
each addition. Mix well. Add extract and coconut mixture;
blend. Pour into pie shell. Bake at 350 degrees for 35 minutes
until firm and golden brown. Serves: 6

Peach Pie

1 8-inch pie shell, unbaked
4 fresh ripe peaches, sliced
⅔ cup sugar
2 tablespoons flour, all-purpose
⅓ cup butter, melted
2 eggs, beaten
½ cup water
2 tablespoons sugar, for top

Place peaches in shell. In a mixing bowl combine sugar, flour,
butter, eggs and water; mix well. Pour mixture over peaches.
Sprinkle sugar. Bake at 400 degrees for 15 minutes; then 50
minutes at 300 degrees. Serves: 6

Fried Fruity Moon Pies

"Easy and fun"

1½ cups sundried fruit bits
1 cup water
½ cup sugar
1 tablespoon butter
¼ teaspoon cinnamon
salt - dash
1 4.5-ounce can biscuits (6)
flour
salt
2 - 3 tablespoons vegetable oil

In small saucepan combine fruit bits with water. Simmer covered on low heat 10 minutes. Add sugar; stir and cook to melt and reduce liquid. Place fruit in blender with butter, cinnamon and salt. Blend thoroughly 2 - 3minutes. Remove fruit from blender and place in small bowl to cool. The consistency should resemble a thick sauce. Roll out one biscuit dough which has been lightly sprinkled with salt on a floured dough board to ⅛ inch thickness. Place 1½ - 2 teaspoons fruit mixture onto rolled out biscuit dough. Fold over dough and pinch edges with a floured fork. Remove uncooked Fruity Moon Pie from dough board and check for any unsealed edge. Prepare other biscuits and place on wax paper until ready to fry. In a skillet heat vegetable oil on medium-high. Add uncooked Fruity Moon Pies and brown each side, turning only once. Remove and drain on paper towels. Yield: 6 pies
Note: "Other dried fruits may be substituted; apricots, apples or peaches. Serve hot or cold. These make wonderful traveling companions."

Lemon Meringue Pie

¼ cup corn starch
3 tablespoons flour, all-purpose
¼ teaspoon salt
1 cup sugar
2 cups water, boiling hot
3 egg yolks, beaten
2 tablespoons butter
6 tablespoons fresh lemon juice
½ teaspoon lemon rind, grated (optional)
1 9-inch pie shell, baked

In a medium sauce pan mix corn starch, flour, salt and sugar. Stir in boiling water. Cook 5 minutes until mixture thickens. Continue stirring and cook 5 more minutes. Remove from heat and blend in butter, juice and rind. Cool. Pour filling into baked shell and top with Scared Stiff Meringue*. Bake at 400 degrees for 10 minutes. Serves: 6

*(See index)

Basic Certified Standard Pastry for Two-Crust

2 cups sifted flour, all-purpose
1 teaspoon salt
¾ cup solid vegetable shortening
4 to 5 tablespoons ice water

Sift flour with salt and cut in shortening using a pastry blender until the mixture resembles coarse cornmeal. Quickly sprinkle water, 1 tablespoon at a time, over all the pastry mixture, tossing lightly with a fork. (Pastry should be just moist enough to hold together, not sticky.) Shape pastry into a ball; wrap in waxed paper, and refrigerate until ready to use. Divide in half; flatten each half with palm of hand and roll out on floured dough board or pastry cloth. Yield: 2 8-inch pie shells

Brown Bag Apple Pie

½ cup sugar
2 tablespoons flour, all-purpose
½ teaspoon nutmeg
4 winesap apples, peeled, cored and cut into ⅛
1 9-inch pie shell, unbaked
2 tablespoons fresh lemon juice

Combine sugar, flour and nutmeg in a small brown bag. Add apples to bag; toss to coat. Pour mixture into pie shell; sprinkle lemon juice. Add topping and slip pie into a brown paper bag. Close, fold up excess and seal with paper clips. Place on a baking sheet and bake at 425 degrees for 1 hour. Serves: 6

Topping:

½ cup sugar
½ cup flour
1 stick butter, cut in small pieces

Combine sugar and flour; sprinkle over apples. Place butter pieces over evenly.

PLANE Vanilla Cream Pie

⅓ cup corn starch
⅔ cup sugar
¼ teaspoon salt
3 cups milk, scalded
3 egg yolks, beaten
2 tablespoons unsalted butter
1½ teaspoons vanilla extract
1 9-inch pie shell, baked

Combine corn starch, sugar and salt in a medium sauce pan. Add milk; stir constantly on medium low heat. Cook and stir until thickened (about 10 minutes). Add egg yolks; cook and stir 5 minutes. Remove from heat; stir in butter and extract. Pour into baked shell. Top with Scared Stiff Meringue*. Lightly brown at 425 degrees. Serves: 6

Alternate: Add 1½ cups flaked coconut for coconut cream pie. Reserve coconut flakes for meringue garnish. Also, use as custard for Banana Pudding.

*(See index)

Lemon Ice Box (2 Pies)

1 12-ounce box vanilla wafers
1 stick butter, melted
3 14-ounce cans sweetened condensed milk
juice of 10 lemons

Place wafers in a plastic bag and roll with a rolling pin until wafers are super fine. Add butter and blend. Divide the crumbs evenly between 2 buttered 8-inch pie pans. Press to form shell. Combine milk with lemon juice; blend. Pour into shells evenly; chill 1 hour. Top with cool whip to serve. Serves: 12

Scared Stiff Meringue

1 tablespoon corn starch
2 tablespoons water, cold
½ cup water, boiling hot
3 egg whites
6 tablespoons sugar
dash salt
½ teaspoon baking powder

Combine corn starch and cold water in a small sauce pan; blend. Stir in boiling water and cook on medium-low heat until clear and thickened; stirring constantly (about 2 minutes). Set aside; cool. Beat egg whites at high speed using an electric mixer and a small bowl. Beat until foamy; gradually add one tablespoon sugar at a time; beating well after each addition. Beat until stiff, but not dry. Beat in salt and baking powder on low speed. Gradually beat in corn starch mixture and extract. Blend well at high speed. Meringue is ready to spread. Yield: approximately 3 cups

Pie In The Sky

Meringue Shell:

> 4 egg whites
> ¼ teaspoon cream of tartar
> 1 cup sugar

Beat egg whites until foamy; add cream of tartar; mix. Gradually add sugar and beat to form stiff peaks. Place on the bottom of an 8 inch buttered pie pan. Bake at 250 degrees for 20 minutes; then 40 minutes at 275 degrees. Set aside and cool. Center will be depressed.

Filling:

> 4 egg yolks, beaten
> ½ cup sugar
> 4 tablespoons lemon juice
> 1 cup whipping cream, whipped

Combine egg yolks, sugar and lemon juice in a double boiler. Stir and cook over low heat until mixture thickens. Cool. Place ½ cup whipped cream in the shell. Spread lemon mixture over the cream and top mixture with the remaining whipped cream. Chill 24 hours before serving. Serves: 6

Strawberry MOONEY Pie

Shell:

>   3 egg yolks
>   ½ cup sugar
>   1½ cups milk
>   ½ teaspoon vanilla extract
>   1 cup white bread cubes
>   2 tablespoons butter, melted

Beat together egg yolks, sugar, milk and extract. Add bread cubes; stir to soak. Pour into a 1½ quart casserole filled with melted butter. Bake at 350 degrees for 45 minutes. Pour warm glaze over warm shell.

Strawberry glaze:

>   ⅔ cup sugar
>   1 tablespoon corn starch
>   1 tablespoon lemon juice
>   3 cups sliced fresh strawberries (1 cup mashed for
>   juice)
>   6 drops red food coloring

Combine sugar and corn starch in a medium sauce pan. Add remaining ingredients. Cook and stir over low heat until thick and glossy. Pour over warm shell. Top with Scared Stiff Meringue*. Brown at 350 degrees for 15 minutes. Serves: 6

*(See index)

Sweet Potato Pie

1 stick butter, melted
½ cup light brown sugar
¼ cup sugar
1½ cups cooked sweet potato, mashed
3 eggs
⅓ cup corn syrup
⅓ cup heavy cream
¼ teaspoon salt
½ teaspoon vanilla extract
½ teaspoon nutmeg
1 9-inch pie shell, unbaked

Using an electric mixer cream butter and sugars well. Add potatoes. Add eggs one at a time; beating well after each addition. In a separate bowl combine syrup, cream, salt, vanilla and nutmeg; blend. Add to potato mixture; blend. Pour into pie shell. Bake at 425 degrees for 10 minutes; then bake at 325 degrees for 45 minutes. Cool before slicing. Serves: 6

Basic Certified Standard Pie Crust

1½ cups flour, all-purpose
½ teaspoon salt
½ cup solid vegetable shortening
3 tablespoons water, cold

Sift dry ingredients and blend in shortening with a pastry blender until the lumps are the size of peas. Add 1 tablespoon water at a time; blending. Roll into a ball, chill until ready to roll. Roll out on pastry cloth or floured dough board into a 10 inch circle. Fit dough into a 9 inch pie pan; flute edges and pierce center with fork before baking. Bake at 400 degrees for 10 minutes.
Yield: 1 9-inch shell

J. B.'s Favorite Persimmon Loaf

1 cup persimmon pulp
⅓ cup milk
1 teaspoon vanilla extract
¾ cup sugar
1 cup flour, all-purpose
½ teaspoon salt
½ teaspoon soda
½ teaspoon cinnamon
½ cup raisins
½ cup black walnuts, chopped coarsely

In a small bowl combine persimmon pulp, milk and vanilla; mix well and set aside. In a large bowl combine sugar, flour, salt, soda, cinnamon, raisins, and nuts; mix well. Combine the two mixtures; mix well. Pour into a greased loaf pan (9 x 5 x 3 inch). Bake at 325 degrees for 50 minutes. Allow to cool in pan. Serve warm or cold. "This recipe has no eggs and no butter." Yield: 1 loaf

"The proof of the pudding
Is in the eating."
Camden, 1623

Over Gross Pecan Pie

1 stick butter
1 cup white Karo
1 cup sugar
4 eggs, beaten
½ teaspoon fresh lemon juice
1 teaspoon vanilla extract
1 dash salt
1 cup pecans, chopped
1 9-inch pie shell, unbaked
10 pecans, whole halves for top

Brown butter in a sauce pan on low heat until light brown. (Do not burn.) In a large mixing bowl combine other ingredients in order listed. Mix well. Stir in browned butter. Mix well. Pour into pie shell, place pecan halves on top for decoration and bake at 425 degrees for 10 minutes; then 325 degrees for 40 minutes. Serves: 6

No Rolling Pie Crust

1½ teaspoons sugar
1½ cups flour, all-purpose
1 teaspoon salt
½ cup vegetable oil
2 tablespoons milk

Combine ingredients and mix well. Press into a 9 inch pie pan. Bake for 10 minutes at 425 degrees.

Rum Cream Pie

1 envelope unflavored gelatin
5 egg yolks
1 cup sugar
⅓ cup dark rum
1½ cups whipping cream
Crumb crust (recipe follows)

Soften gelatin in ½ cup cold water. Place over low heat and bring almost to a boil, stirring to dissolve. Beat egg yolks and sugar until very light. Stir gelatin into egg yolk mixture, cool. Gradually add rum, beating constantly. Whip cream until it stands in soft peaks and fold into gelatin mixture. Cool until mixture begins to set, then spoon onto crumb crust and chill until firm. Grated chocolate may be sprinkled on top as a garnish.

Crumb Crust

2¼ cups graham cracker crumbs
½ cup butter, melted
2 tablespoons sugar
½ teaspoon cinnamon

Combine ingredients and press into a 9-inch pie pan. Chill until filling is ready.

the
HISTORIC
FARNSWORTH
HOUSE

HHH
HHH

BUILT 1810
401 Baltimore Street
Gettysburg, PA 17325   (717) 334-8838

Chocolate Cream Pie

4 tablespoons flour, all-purpose
1 cup sugar
3 tablespoons cocoa
1½ cups heavy cream
4 egg yolks, beaten
3 tablespoons butter
1 teaspoon vanilla extract
1 9-inch baked pie shell

Combine flour, sugar and cocoa in a medium sauce pan. Slowly add cream. Stirring constantly cook on medium-low heat until mixture thickens. Add egg yolks; cook 5 minutes. Remove from heat and blend in butter and extract; cool. Pour into shell and top with Scared Stiff Meringue*. Brown at 400 degrees about 10 minutes. Serves: 6
*(See index)

Ritz Pie

26 Ritz crackers
1 cup pecans, chopped finely
3 egg whites
1 cup sugar
1 teaspoon vanilla extract
½ pint whipping cream, whipped
nutmeg

Place crackers in a plastic bag and roll with a rolling pin until super fine or spin in food processor. Combine with nuts. Beat the egg whites stiff. Beat in sugar well; add extract. Fold egg mixture into cracker mixture. Pour into a buttered 8-inch pie pan. Bake at 350 degrees for 25 minutes. Cool. Top with whipped cream and a few nutmeg dashes. Serves: 6

Persimmon Pudding

2 cups persimmon pulp
1½ cups flour, all-purpose
1¼ cups sugar
1 teaspoon baking soda
1 teaspoon baking powder
½ teaspoon salt
2 teaspoons cinnamon
½ teaspoon nutmeg
1 teaspoon ginger
2½ cups rich cream or milk
3 eggs, beaten
1 stick butter, melted

Press persimmons through a colander to render pulp. Pulp may be frozen for use during barren months. Combine dry ingredients and pulp; stir in milk, eggs and butter. Pour into a 9 x 9 inch baking dish (buttered). Bake at 325 degrees for 1 hour and 10 minutes. Serve hot or cold. (Skim milk may be substituted.)
Serves: 10

Regulation Crumb Crust

1¼ cups crumbs, crushed finely (wafers or sweet
    crackers)
¼ cup sugar
¼ cup butter, melted

Combine all ingredients in a plastic bag; toss and blend. Press firmly over bottom and sides of a 9 inch pie pan. Chill for 1 hour and bake at 375 degrees for 8 minutes. Yield 1 9-inch shell

– *Notes* –

DESSERTS

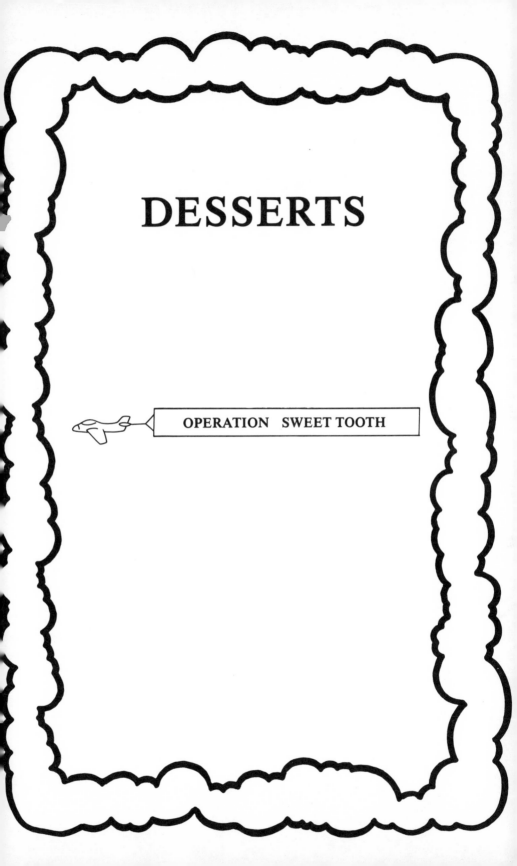

OPERATION   SWEET TOOTH

Chocolate Mousse

1½ cups walnuts, chopped super finely
1 tablespoon white vinegar
1 tablespoon water
6 egg whites
1 12-ounce package semi-sweet chocolate morsels
3 tablespoons cocoa
½ cup sugar
1½ sticks butter, unsalted (melted and boiling hot)
4 egg yolks

Butter bottom and sides of a 1 quart glass loaf pan. Line bottom with parchment paper; butter paper. Press nuts into bottom and sides. Combine vinegar and water in a small bowl. Beat egg whites until stiff, but not dry; add vinegar mixture and set aside. Using a food processor, combine chocolate, cocoa and sugar; process until fine. Add hot butter; process 1 minute. Scrape down sides and add egg yolks; process 10 seconds. Add egg white mixture and process 4 seconds. Spoon mousse into prepared pan. Cover with plastic wrap and refrigerate 3 hours. May be frozen at this time and held for 1 month if desired. To serve, invert onto serving platter and slice. Serves: 8 - 10

"Outrageously Delicious"

Clouds

3 eggs, separated
2 cups milk
⅛ teaspoon salt
¼ cup sugar
1 teaspoon lemon extract, almond or vanilla

Beat egg yolks until foamy. Place in sauce pan with milk, salt and sugar. Cook on medium-low heat; stirring until slightly thickened (about 10 minutes). Remove from heat and add flavoring. Cool. Beat egg whites until stiff, but not dry. Fold into mixture and pour into footed glass containers. Chill until serving. Serves: 4

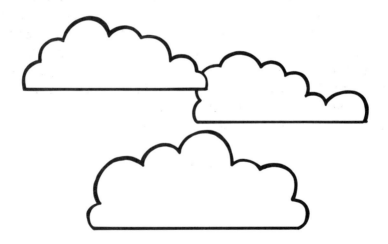

Apple Crisp

8 medium apples, peeled, cored and sliced
2 cups sugar
1⅛ cups flour
1¾ tablespoons cinnamon, divided
2 tablespoons butter
1 teaspoon baking powder
½ teaspoon salt
1 egg

Blend apples with ¾ tablespoon cinnamon, one cup sugar and two tablespoons flour. Place in buttered baking dish and dot with butter. Mix one cup sugar, one cup sifted flour, baking powder, salt, one egg and one tablespoon cinnamon until crumbly. Sprinkle over the apples and bake at 350 degrees until bubbly and brown. Serve warm with whipped cream or ice cream, if desired.

EVANS FARM INN

1696 Chain Bridge Road McLean, Virginia 22101-4398
703-356-8000

Maria and Ralph Evans
Keepers of the Inn

Café de lay Ice Cream

½ cup water, cold
½ cup cognac
2 tablespoons instant coffee
1 quart rich vanilla ice cream, soft
nutmeg

Combine all ingredients except nutmeg in a blender; blend until smooth. Chill in freezer until mushy; (about 2 hours). Stir before serving. Scoop into brandy snifters and sprinkle nutmeg lightly.
Serves: 4

Strawberry Malibu Delight

2 6-ounce packages strawberry gelatin
2½ cups water, boiling hot
1 pint whipping cream, whipped
2 10-ounce packages frozen strawberries, thawed
¼ teaspoon salt
1 8-inch angel food cake, brown crust removed
3 fresh strawberries, garnish

Dissolve gelatin in boiling water. Freeze until partially set (about 25 minutes). Beat gelatin and fold in whipped cream; mix in strawberries and salt; set aside. Grate the cake. Layer ½ of the cake in a 4 quart oiled mold. Pour ½ of the gelatin mixture over the cake; repeat ending with gelatin on top. Cover and chill 5 hours. To serve, garnish with fresh strawberry slices. Serves: 8

SOP Sherbet

2 eggs, separated
4 tablespoons fresh lemon juice
⅜ cup pineapple juice
⅜ cup raw honey
1¼ cups milk

Beat the egg yolks well. Combine fruit juices with honey; stir to blend. Slowly pour the juice mixture over the egg yolks. Gradually add the milk. Beat well. Pour into a 1½ quart mold. Freeze to a soft mush (about 1½ hours). Beat the egg whites until they form stiff peaks. Fold in the egg whites and freeze until set. Stir several times while freezing. Serves: 4

NO SKIDDING -
Delicious Sweet Pears

4 large pears
16 ounces sauterne
1 cup sugar
1 egg yolk, beaten
3 ounces whipping cream
½ teaspoon vanilla extract
⅛ teaspoon all spice

Wash and peel pears using a potato peeler without removing the stems. Combine the sauterne and sugar; bring to a boil. Add the pears and cook for 20 minutes on low heat turning them gently for uniform cooking. Remove pears from syrup and cool. Reserve syrup. Combine egg yolk, cream, extract and all spice and add to syrup. Cook over low heat, stirring constantly until it starts to boil. Remove from heat and pour over pears. Chill and serve cold. Serves: 4

"Elegantly Delicious"

Persimmon Ice Cream

4 large ripe persimmons
2 tablespoons sugar
6 tablespoons fresh lemon juice
2 cups whipping cream
nutmeg

Wash persimmons and strain; reserve pulp. Dissolve sugar in lemon juice. Whip cream until thick, but not stiff. Combine pulp, lemon mixture and cream; mix well. Pour into a 2 quart mold and freeze. Sprinkle with nutmeg to serve. Serves: 4

Mile High Pie

Crust:

⅓ cup butter, melted
1¼ cups graham cracker crumbs

Combine butter and cracker crumbs; mix well. Press firmly into an 8 inch pie pan. Bake at 350 degrees for 5 minutes. Chill.

Filling:

1 quart rich ice cream, your favorite flavor, soft

Fill crust with ice cream and freeze.

Topping:

1 recipe Scared Stiff Meringue*. Spread evenly and cover pie completely. May be returned to freezer at this point. To serve: place pie on a baking sheet with the shiny side down. Bake at 500 degrees until lightly browned (about 4 minutes). Serve immediately with Hot Fudge Sauce. Serves: 6

*(See index)

Hot Fudge Sauce

1 cup whipping cream
2 teaspoons butter
dash salt
1 4-ounce package German chocolate
1 teaspoon vanilla extract

Combine cream, butter, salt and chocolate in top of double boiler. Cook on medium heat until chocolate is melted; stir to blend. Mix in extract. Serve hot or refrigerate. Reheats easily in microwave. Yield: approximately 1 cup

The Frisco Fluff

Melt ¼ pound of butter in small sauce pan over low heat. Add 1 cup of flour slowly and make a golden roux. Add to 9 x 13 inch bake pan and spread thinly over bottom of pan. Sprinkle 5 ounces of crushed pecans onto pan. Press firmly into flour roux. Put in oven at 350 degrees for 10 minutes.

While crust is cooling, prepare bottom layer. 8 ounces of Philadelphia cream cheese, 12 ounces of Cool Whip and one cup of sugar. Mix very well, then spread evenly over crust.

Second layer. Open can of crushed pineapple and drain juices very well. Mix 6½-ounce box of instant vanilla pudding with 3 cups of milk. Mix well then add pineapple. Mix well again. Put in freezer for 2 minutes so pudding will firm up. Then spread evenly over bottom layer.

For third layer, take 12 ounces of Cool Whip and spread evenly over second layer. Wave top, then sprinkle generously with crushed coconut.

Put in freezer to firm, then put in refrigerator while in use. Do not use frozen.

Del Frisco's
U.S.D.A. PRIME
Steak House
2501 Canal St.
New Orleans, LA 70119

Milky Way Ice Cream

8 Milky Way Bars
1 cup heavy cream
2 cups milk
6 eggs, beaten
2 cups sugar
2 tablespoons vanilla extract
2 12-ounce cans evaporated milk

Combine Milky Way Bars, heavy cream and milk in medium saucepan; melt and blend on low heat. Cool. Beat eggs with sugar well; add evaporated milk and extract. Combine the two mixtures; mix well. Pour into 4 quart ice cream container and freeze. Yield: 4 quarts

Drifts of Heaven

1 8-ounce cream cheese
1 can peach pie filling
1 cup milk
¼ cup powdered sugar
1 9-ounce cool whip
1 8-inch angel food cake, brown crust removed

Combine cream cheese, pie filling, milk and sugar in a blender; mix well. Fold in one-half of the cool whip. Grate the cake or spin in a food processor. Layer ⅓ cake in a buttered 13 x 9 x 2 inch container. Layer ⅓ of the cheese mixture. Continue layers ending with the cheese mixture. Top with remaining cool whip. Chill 8 hours. Serve chilled. Serves: 8

Restaurants Listed by State
for easy reference

CALIFORNIA

La Brasserie
202 South Main Street
Orange, California
(714) 639-7264

FLORIDA

The DoNut Hole
635 Highway 98 East
Destin, Florida 32541
(904) 837-8874

Chalet Suzanne Restaurant and Country Inn
U. S. 27 North
Lake Wales, Florida
(813) 676-6011

The Hopkins' House, Inc.
900 North Spring Street
Pensacola, Florida 32501
(904) 456-1121

LOUISIANA

Willy Coln's Chalet
2505 Whitney Avenue
Gretna, Louisiana 70056
(504) 361-3860

Willy Coln's Kaleidoscope
Canal Place – 3rd Level
New Orleans, Louisiana 70130

Del Frisco's Steak House
2501 Canal Street
New Orleans, Louisiana 70119
(504) 821-8811

Leon's Smoked Turkey
4723 Monkhouse Drive
Shreveport, Louisiana 71109
(318) 635-5700
Also East Kings Highway location

NEW YORK

The Captain's Table
860 Second Avenue, Corner of 46th Street
New York, New York 10017
(212) 697-9538

NEBRASKA

The Renaissance
Cornhusker Hotel
333 South 13th Street
Lincoln, Nebraska 68508
(402) 474-7474

NEVADA

Philips Supper House
4545 West Sahara Avenue
Las Vegas, Nevada 89102
(702) 873-5222

NORTH CAROLINA

High Hampton Inn and Country Club
Cashiers, North Carolina 28717
(704) 743-2411

PENNSYLVANIA

The Historic Farnsworth House
401 Baltimore Street
Gettysburg, Pennsylvania 17325
(717) 334-8838

Restaurant La Normande
5030 Centre Avenue
Pittsburgh, Pennsylvania 15213
(412) 621-0744

RHODE ISLAND

Red Rooster Tavern
7385 Post Road
North Kingston, Rhode Island 02852
(401) 295-8804

The White Horse Tavern
Corner of Marlborough and Farewell Streets
Newport, Rhode Island 02840
(401) 849-3600

TEXAS

Del Frisco Steak House
4300 Lemmon Avenue
Dallas, Texas 75219
(214) 526-2101

Charley's 517
517 Louisiana
Houston, Texas
(713) 224-4438

VERMONT

Hemingway's Restaurant
Kellington, Vermont
(802) 422-3886

VIRGINIA

Evans Farm Inn
1696 Chain Bridge Road
McLean, Virginia 22101-4398
(703) 356-8000

WASHINGTON

Calgary Steak House
East 3040 Sprague Avenue
Spokane, Washington 99202
(509) 535-7502

The restaurants listed were invited to be a part of **The Flying Gourmet** without charge because they are convenient for pilots and are known for their good food and hospitality. Please refer to the index for recipes of their specialties.

223

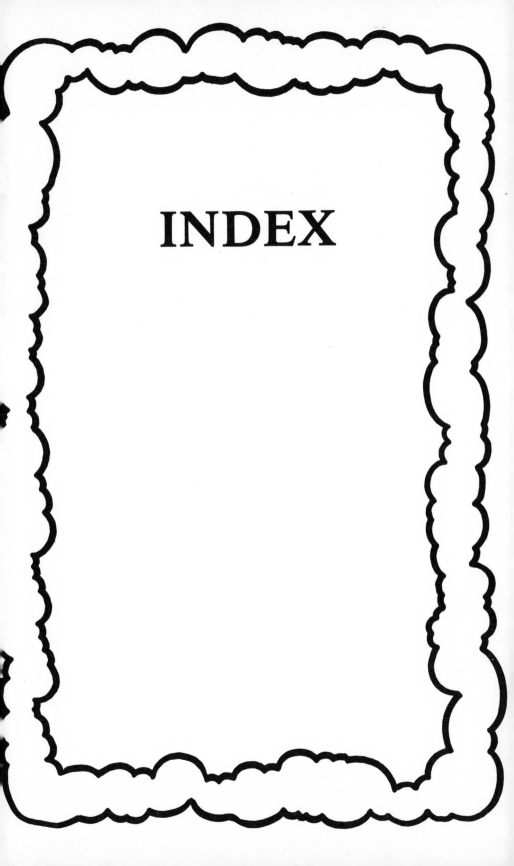

INDEX

INDEX

A

B

INDEX

INDEX

INDEX

INDEX

P

Pancakes

Pasta

Peas

Persimmon

Pickles

Pie Crust

Pies

Pineapple

Pork

Potatoes (See also Sweet Potatoes)

Pound Cakes

Q

R

S

INDEX

M & M Publications
P. O. Box 15301
New Orleans, LA 70115

Please send _____ copy(ies) of *The Flying Gourmet* cookbook at $14.95 per copy, plus $1.95 per copy for mailing. Louisiana residents include 4% sales tax plus local tax. Add $1.00 for each desired gift wrapping.

Name _____

Address _____

City _____ State _____ Zip _____

	Visa ☐ Master Card ☐	Autograph To
Card # _____		_____
Expiration date _____		_____
Cardholder's name _____		_____

M & M Publications
P. O. Box 15301
New Orleans, LA 70115

Please send _____ copy(ies) of *The Flying Gourmet* cookbook at $14.95 per copy, plus $1.95 per copy for mailing. Louisiana residents include 4% sales tax plus local tax. Add $1.00 for each desired gift wrapping.

Name _____

Address _____

City _____ State _____ Zip _____

	Visa ☐ Master Card ☐	Autograph To
Card # _____		_____
Expiration date _____		_____
Cardholder's name _____		_____